# ENTREPRENEURIAL
# INSANITY

# IN THE HOMECARE BUSINESS

## When Doing the Same Things Does Not Produce Different Results

Tim Rowan
Roger McManus

Rich,
Enjoy!

Tim Rowan

ENTREPRENEURIAL INSANITY
IN THE HOMECARE BUSINESS
When Doing the Same Things Does Not
Produce Different Results ...

Copyright © 2017 by EnSanity Press

Printed in USA                                      1.4

# Dedications

This book is dedicated to my many teachers. I have met you in classrooms, seminars, books and tapes. I have experienced you in success and failure; victories and disappointments. I have collected your wisdom, tested your lessons, enjoyed your approval and suffered your reproach. I seek only to be worthy of passing on your wisdom through my interpretation of your lessons.

And, not ever to be forgotten when you look at how it all gets put together, however, is my most patient and consistent teacher, advisor, consultant, editor and friend, my wife, Patsy.

~ Roger McManus

Everyone has a mentor, someone more experienced, perhaps a little older, who appears just at the right time and shares his wisdom. I am able to co-author this book with some authority because I had a great one. Tom Williams was an outside-the-box thinker who knew Healthcare at Home from deep inside. Before we went into business together, he was the VP of Government Services for the company known today as NGS, a Medicare Administrative Contractor. A renowned story-teller, Tom brought me into his world, from technology to marketing to politics, until I knew it as well as he did. Though he left us too soon, my ten years under his tutelage equipped me to step into his shoes and continue to serve home health, home care and hospice providers with the same infectious passion and enthusiasm that characterized his life.

~ Tim Rowan

# THE AUTHORS

## Tim Rowan

Tim has been in home health care since 1993, first as CIO of a Colorado agency, then as an industry analyst and reporter. For ten years, he apprenticed under the late Tom Williams, the most highly regarded technology expert home care and hospice has ever known.

Now, as principal of Rowan Consulting Associates, he focuses his activities on educating an entire industry as publisher of the *Home Care Technology Report*, a weekly online newsletter he has shaped and managed since 1998, and as a trusted advisor to home healthcare providers and hospices needing to make substantial investments in software.

After years of studying the home care technology market, Tim is in a unique position to guide technology vendor selection through a proven strategic process. Interviews with key staff to familiarize himself with agency operations and culture enable identification of a handful of likely technology partners, eliminating the need for managers to interview dozens of candidates. This process saves agencies thousands of dollars and hours trying to find the best vendor on their own -- and tens of thousands over making the wrong selection.

# Roger McManus

For well over 30 years, Roger McManus has coached, funded, counseled and published for entrepreneurs. As a serial entrepreneur, he has garnered the wisdom of dozens of advisers and gathered years of experiences in his effort to develop a clear picture of the entrepreneurial mindset.

In this understanding, Roger has dived deeply into the Homecare industry and garnered the cooperation of some of its greatest players. The result is a book that promises to offer those in the Homecare business a new look at what is probably a very established business.

As a magazine publisher, speaker, author and consultant, McManus has had the rare opportunity to see inside businesses resulting in the conclusion that many call themselves entrepreneurs, but few truly achieve the levels of freedom that the title should imply.

Recognized by the SBA as Media Advocate of the Year and elected to the White House Conference on Small Business, McManus takes the plight and the opportunities of the small business owner to heart in his writing. The Entrepreneurial Insanity series explores how changing the point of view, plus the development of a few systems can deliver the objective of business ownership: freedom for the owner to work less in the business while deriving greater value from it.

# Table of Contents

# INTRODUCTION

## From Insanity to Independence

This book is the product of the combined experience of a serial entrepreneur and a publisher. They say that experience is the best teacher. We are well educated.

This book is the product of observation. Roger has had the good fortune to work with hundreds of different business owners, observing the patterns. Tim has "walked the walk" from working with single unit up to billion dollar corporations with thousands of locations across the country. To accomplish this book, we blended our experiences to deliver a powerful message to those who make their living in the Healthcare at Home business. Our goal is to make it more than just your living.

This book is the product of disappointment. We have each experienced ourselves and observed the bright dreams of would-be entrepreneurs who remained small business owners; people who never stopped owning a job instead of building an asset.

This book is the product of inspiration. It came about as a result of one of those "Aha!" moments when all that we had experienced academically came rushing forward to become reality. That "Aha!" can actually be summed up in a single statement:

Those who start businesses rarely think of their venture as an investment; they just want to own something that will provide them with a job.

This book is the product of accumulation. Over the years Roger published magazines for small business owners, was involved with trade organizations large and small and consulted with larger corporations; he accumulated the experiences and stories that made the idea behind Entrepreneurial Insanity possible. Entrepreneurial Insanity in the Homecare Business combines his experiences with those of Tim who adds greater depth and tenure to the subject. The blend results in powerful guidance.

This book is the product of an Objective. If this book does its job, it will move you, the owner of an independent restaurant, catering operation, or small restaurant group into an entrepreneur's mindset. Your definition of "the healthcare at home business" will be altered forever. It will shift your motivation from making a living to developing an asset. It will move you from the position of being in business to being exactly like the money suppliers you may have approached. Money suppliers, you see, do not care about owning a business; they care about creating a saleable asset – and making a profit.

When the owner of a healthcare at home business focuses on the goal of establishing the enterprise as a salable entity – whether he or she actually sells it or not – there is a massive shift in intention and attention. From that point, every decision has at its core whether it is good for the enterprise as an entity separate from the owner.

The metamorphosis from restaurant business owner to entrepreneur is the process of ending the insanity with which so many owners of healthcare at home businesses suffer today. This book is the product of "entrepreneurial insanity."

# SECTION ONE: Choosing Freedom

## CHAPTER 1

# Are You Involved or Insane?

*Work harder !*
*Work smarter, not harder !*
*Concentrate !*
*Focus your attention !*
*Know the regs !*
*Motivate your people !*
*Plan your day !*

Over the years, you have heard them all. They may be apt admonitions for football teams and high school students but working, concentrating, focusing, motivating and planning are only useful if they are accomplished within a larger picture.

Let's refer to that larger picture as **The Objective**.

It is your constant attempts to do better by working harder that creates insanity. Albert Einstein contributed the definition of Insanity that is so often quoted, that most of us have it memorized: ***"Doing the same thing over and over again and expecting different results."***

How perfectly this defines how most businesses are operated today! Too many small business owners obey the seven admonitions that opened this chapter and believe that, as a result, they can succeed – if they just try harder.

The Pennsylvania Dutch phrase, "The hurrier I go, the behinder I get" applies equally. Working harder – or hurrier – does not achieve The Objective.

The Objective (capitalized because it is the Holy Grail in this text) is as simple as answering the question, "What do you want to get out of this business you have started?" Or, better yet, "How do you get out of this business you find yourself in?"

## The Objective

It is not enough to say "make a living" or, more generally, "make money." Money is not The Objective. It is the fuel. It is a good measuring tape but it is not The Objective.

Ask any truly aware entrepreneur why he or she has his or her own business and the answer always boils down to some variation of the word "freedom." Sure, money buys you freedom, but having money does not make you free. Ask the owner of an amazingly successful retail store who is making money hand-over-fist, but has to be in his store 100 hours a week to make it happen. Money? Yes. Freedom? Hardly! This is a shame because (cue drumroll), *Freedom* is The Objective.

Conversely, unless the business produces money, freedom is not even possible. So, yes, it is about money, but it is not only about money. The quest for freedom ought to begin before the business is even open. If the business is already open – as I suspect is the case with most people reading this book – then the quest for freedom starts today.

A large percentage of today's home care agency owners are nurses who started as employees of other agencies and decided to strike out on their own. They are spinoff entrepreneurs. Their choice was to move from employee to owner but there is a danger that all they have done is bought themselves a different job or, more accurately perhaps, the same job at a different address.

Either way, the quest for freedom is just the same, often stronger. Gen Two always has new ideas that Gen One had no interest or inclination in pursuing. As Gen Two begins to separate from "the way things were done at my last agency," new ways of thinking and an openness to try new technologies and institute new procedures make whole new ways of thinking and new paths to growth possible.

As you will learn in these pages, the path to freedom is built entirely on growth. Not more patients, though larger census is a by-product of growth, but true growth. Hint of advice to come: True growth is not possible if the owner insists on being the only wound care nurse in the agency!

The path to freedom starts today as you read the first few chapters in this book. It starts as you feel your mind moving from "doing" to "strategizing" and from "strategizing" to "executing." The execution of the quest for The Objective will deliver to you the benefits that so many people who start (or inherit) businesses really want but, so few achieve. Our work together, as you move through this text, will empower you to actually achieve The Objective.

## A Warning

This process may not make you more popular. Some of your loyal employees will not seem so loyal as you make hard decisions, institute new rules and demand accountability. Others will understand and relish the responsibilities with which you will entrust them. Train yourself to recognize the difference.

Inevitably, you will not end up with the same staff as when you started this process. It simply cannot happen unless you are starting from scratch – and, even then, there will be people you thought would be a part of your long-term team who will not make it through the process.

Those who will make it through the transition will be happier and more productive. Along the way everyone will have acquired a roadmap that gives employees more autonomy and gives you more freedom.

## A Happy Possibility

This process will make you more popular with your family, however, as long as you gently guide them to understand and buy into The Objective.

Even the strongest family relationship is strained when one member of the family has a lover outside the family. Your "lover" is the business. The impression that your focus is always elsewhere (which you may justify because you are working so hard for the family) is a strain on love relationships and loving involvement with your children. All too often, committed small business owners (who just think they are entrepreneurs) assume that the family understands. While that may be logically true, and while they may give lip service to that understanding, it is rarely emotionally true.

Perhaps your interest was piqued by my parenthetical comment "who just think they are entrepreneurs." In the pages to come, you will become acutely aware of the difference between owning a business and being an entre-preneur. In fact, the entire first three chapters are devoted to making that difference abundantly clear.

This book is not designed to make you comfortable. It will be most successful if it turns your world upside down. The objective of this book is not to change what you do – there are thousands of books that will tell you what to do – nor to tell you what to think. The objective of this book is to offer you a pattern of thought that is dramatically different from that of 98 percent of small business owners today – and perhaps an even greater percentage of your colleagues in the Healthcare at Home business!

You are certainly familiar with the examples of small businesses that became massive companies, such as LHC Group, Kindred or Home Instead. While no one who picks up this text is guaranteed to own a multi-million dollar corporation as a result, anyone who adjusts his or her thinking in their approach to what they are doing will experience a shift in awareness that will yield extremely positive results and, hopefully, achieve The Objective – your freedom from running the business and (finally) to experience the joy of owning an asset.

# CHAPTER 2

# Are You a Small Business Owner or an Entrepreneur?

It is fun to call yourself an entrepreneur. The French word slips off the tongue and has an elegance about it that sounds so much better than "small business owner." So, without recrimination, many small business owners like to call themselves entrepreneurs even if they have not earned the designation. Owners of home health, home care or hospice organizations who call themselves entrepreneurs are not necessarily deluding themselves, they are usually merely wrong.

The difference between entrepreneurism and small business ownership is night and day. It is not unlike the difference between a cook and a chef. Truth be known, there are not very many true chefs in the entire world. There are millions of cooks, many of whom call themselves chefs. It is not deceptive, just incorrect.

This is not merely an issue of semantics. The person who considers herself to be a great cook – maybe even a great chef – often thinks that such skill is sufficient to open a restaurant. She knows how to do the preparation; why not create a business around what she loves to do?

The home care agency owner who understands clinical assessments, medication management, and how to give a patient a bath can be a successful agency owner. These skills, however, are not the ones needed to achieve The Objective.

## The Difference

The critical difference between being skilled at cooking and being skilled at running a restaurant is dramatic! Knowing the right amount of ingredients in the goulash is very different from balancing inventory and managing vendors, staffing the front and back of the house, grasping all of the various regulatory requirements, making payroll, paying rent, keeping a liquor license, setting menu prices, and dancing with the health inspector.

Often, the entrepreneur who owns a successful restaurant does not even know how to cook all that well!

The critical difference between being a skilled clinician and being skilled at running a home healthcare business is equally dramatic. Knowing how to foresee and treat a CHF exacerbation is very different from managing payroll and inventory, advertising and bookkeeping, handling hazardous waste correctly and negotiating contracts with managed care companies.

As in our restaurant analogy, it is quite possible that the entrepreneur who owns a highly successful in-home care business would never consider dressing an open wound!

Even should the business owner also be an experienced nurse or therapist, the title "entrepreneur" still may not apply. Perhaps "manager" or the term used in this text, "overseer," but not entrepreneur.

"Entrepreneur" is the honorific conferred when all of the detail of running the business is codified in a series of systems and recorded in an Operations Manual that is so clear that the owner is not needed at all. This is when the owner gains the freedom to study new profit centers, acquire new locations or spend time promoting a larger community image through involvement with the Chamber of Commerce or state home care association, for example.

Perhaps the easiest way to make the distinction is to use the example of a hamburger stand – no chefs involved here! The small business owner of a hamburger stand decides that he wants to grow. The quickest and easiest way to grow is to put coupons in the paper and a sign in the window advertising discounted hamburgers (or bigger ones, or tastier ones, or hamburgers made 100 different ways). He uses all of his marketing resources to generate more sales. The entrepreneur, on the other hand, expends his resources in an effort to *open more restaurants*. He knows the first hamburger stand will operate just fine without him on a day-to-day basis because he has already established systems that replace him. (Much more about systems to come.)

It is a matter of scale. It is a matter of mindset. It is the difference between growing sales and growing the business.

The entrepreneur understands that when he grows the business, he is no longer selling hamburgers. He is developing business systems. Ultimately, if they are successful, he can sell those business systems, perhaps as a franchise. He never loses sight of the fact that, though he might be selling hamburger restaurant business systems, he is never selling hamburgers.

It is absolutely the only mindset through which an individual can ever open a second location – or more – and survive financially (or emotionally).

Remember the hamburger stand analogy and you are on your way toward mastering the Entrepreneurial Insanity concept. The thesis of this book, to which we will return until you are hearing it in your sleep, is that entrepreneurism is a mindset that triggers entirely different behaviors than those required of a small business owner. Our objective is to help the reader redefine entrepreneurism and, as a consequence, take a different path toward small business ownership. If you are reading this book before you open your business, even better. You may be able to jump over a few painful steps that bogged down your competitors.

## Growth

The entrepreneur is defined by a single guiding principal – growth. He understands that he has limited personal capacity, no matter how skilled he might be. To grow, he must have people; and he knows those people will not always be the most brilliant, forward-thinking, goal-minded individuals. If they were, they would be running their own home healthcare agency. No, the entrepreneur understands that normal people, well, let's say it, unexceptional people, will be the backbone of his enterprises. What the entrepreneur brings to the party is a vision and a system.

That is not to say that the entrepreneur does not seek the help and counsel of talented people. The smartest entrepreneurs hire people more skilled than themselves and have the maturity to know what they do not know. But, for the majority of the people who are working in your business on a day-to-day basis, it is folly to think that they are going to be consistently above average, even with the best screening and hiring systems. The most secure way to plan around this probability is to develop business systems that are "ability neutral;" systems that a properly hired and trained individual can execute because they are clear and easy to understand and follow. We will explore this topic extensively in the following pages.

## Different Skills

By way of further clarifying the difference between entrepreneur and small business owner, think about the inherent skill set that an entrepreneur brings to the table that is distinctly different from someone who is inclined to simply open a business. The entrepreneur is a creator, not a manager. The entrepreneur is happy to (and better off to) create the business, develop it as an organized and profitable entity, sell it and move on. Entrepreneurs who stay on too long will find themselves becoming bored with the project – regardless of how successful it is – and actually hamper the business by sticking around. Those who stay too long tend to get fired by their investors.

The Generation Two entrepreneur is no less a creator, even though her spinoff business may have been modeled after the one she left. Once the Gen Two owner has left the nest, the new creation can take many forms – any of which can lead to The Objective. The Gen Two owner's responsibility is to move her own business from a place to work, which is no more than what she had before, to an asset that can be sold – whether or not she elects to do so.

Where the entrepreneur successfully stays with the business he started is when he uses his inherent creative skill set to expand the business within the niche in which it was built originally. That is how a single home health agency spawns a group of branches, acquires a hospice, or opens a private duty division which, in turn, begins to open its own branch locations and establishes itself as a brand separate from Kindred, Home Instead or Almost Family.

A great example of this is Great Lakes Cares Home Health and Hospice in Jackson, Michigan, where William Deary, a veteran of the textbook publishing industry, took his nurse wife's suggestion and started a small certified home health agency in 1998. As he managed the business and his wife managed patient care, the tiny enterprise began to grow.

Soon, William found he had the wherewithal to acquire a neighboring agency, then another, and another, until today when he oversees a statewide umbrella corporation, with multiple branch offices, that recently began to expand into Ohio, Illinois, Indiana and Massachusetts.

William personifies the path from small business owner to entrepreneur. Ask him the secret of his success, however, and he will insist that all the credit goes to his staff. Having wisely hired and trained a staff he can trust to run the business and given them guidelines to follow, William Deary is free.

It should be noted that doing everything in this book will not convert you magically from being a small home care business owner to being William Deary. It will give you a path to follow that is often taken by entrepreneurs. It is our hope, however, that you will be thunderstruck by the realization that there is a large and dramatic difference between running a business (a job) and owning a business (entrepreneurism).

Once that mental conversion has occurred, the path to opening additional businesses becomes possible, because all the new businesses are approached in a much different way than the first. Even if you do not jump on the growth bandwagon, business ownership will become a much more pleasant experience.

Where the small business owner often gets stuck goes back to the reason he or she opened the business to begin with. Very often the small business owner comes from the corporate environment where there are structures and rules and all sorts of independence-quashing factors they have come to live with and resent. One day the decision to quit is made – or the job is taken away. The "silver lining" around the dark cloud of a job loss is the new opportunity to throw off the burden of corporate limitations and seek what is seen as "freedom" to now make all of the decisions.

All too often however, the new-found "freedom" is the freedom to decide which 80 hours to work each week.

## Job Mentality

Unfortunately, many new small business owners bring the "job" mentality right into the business. They know how to do the task and it becomes their "job" to do it. Employees are hired to help them do the job. Growing means doing more of the job. The more of the job that gets done, the more money the small business person makes. That does work – for a while.

Eventually, however, the job that was so unappealing in the corporate environment is twice or three times as large now that it is being done for yourself. There are longer days and fewer days off. Relief comes with the cost of higher payroll and the job is never done as well as when the owner did it himself. All of this freedom becomes a burden. Life is eaten up by the obligation. It stops being fun. Sometimes it becomes terrifying. (See Chapter 7 for more on the topic of Entrepreneurial Terror.)

The entrepreneur knows how to avoid being caught in this terror. The small business owner creates his job and gets things done by working hard and hiring help when he needs it. The entrepreneur creates an enterprise that gets things done through him, not by him. He has the power to create, more than the desire to do. He has a growth mentality.

The entrepreneur succeeds or fails based on the strength of ideas and systems. The small business owner succeeds or fails based on the limits of personal stamina. All too often the business kills – spiritually if not literally – the owner who started it.

Therein lies the invitation to change. To make the move from a position that Michael Gerber described in the E-Myth as working in the business to one of working on the business; from being a small business owner to becoming an entrepreneur. Therein lies the path to The Objective.

# CHAPTER 3

# Do You Own an Asset or a Job You Cannot Quit?

You have had it with the job – or the job is now gone. Either way, you have decided to make it on your own. You are going to start a business. You will be the boss. You will control your own destiny. You will achieve the freedom (that word!) that you could never have when working for someone else. It is a thrilling time!

So you create a place to go to work. You create a Job. Your company, Job, Inc., becomes the place you go to do your work. You go to your Job.

Even though this is only Chapter 3, you can already sense the trap, can't you? You have not created a business; you have created a Job. The Job is what you do. It is what you know how to do. It is what you do to make money. It may be very much like the job you left before you created The Job. Or, it might be very different. But, almost certainly, it is something you know.

It happens millions of times each year. Displaced or displeased employees become "entrepreneurs" to create a Job to replace their old employment. They tell their families, friends and themselves that they are "starting a new business" when, in fact, they are starting a new "Job."

## The Difference

What is the difference between owning a business and owning a Job?

The business is a living, breathing thing that the owner creates for the purpose of building an independent entity that sustains the owner until which time it has matured to the point that it can be sold as a profitable investment.

A Job is an entity created by the owner to make money for himself – and to have something to *do*! It rarely has a plan. It rarely has a defined objective beyond cash flow. It very rarely provides the freedom the creator thought it would. It can rarely be sold for more that the physical assets and salable inventory, which in the Healthcare at Home business can be pretty minimal.

You see it all the time. Ads in *Entrepreneur* magazine are replete with these opportunities to buy a piece of equipment and be in the carpet cleaning *business* or the windshield repair *business* or the locksmith *business*. They are all jobs. Many do not require any labor beyond that of the owner of the *business*.

Consider the hairstylist who works in someone else's salon gets what Gerber called in *The E-Myth* an "entrepreneurial seizure" and opens her own beauty salon. It is unlikely that this newborn entrepreneur gave a second thought to the distinction between styling hair and running the *business* of styling hair.

Dental schools do a great job of preparing Doctors of Dental Surgery (DDS) to practice medicine. However, they do very little to teach the *business* of dentistry. Think about the range of skills, having nothing to do with dental medicine, that are necessary to establishing a dental practice that is economically viable. Few dentists graduate and open a "store." They join practices with other dentists or they occasionally buy existing practices where the staff teaches the new owner the *business* of dentistry. But, you can see the distinct difference between medicine and creating a business.

Perhaps your home care business was in your family and your *job* is a foregone conclusion. Eventual ownership is assumed, still moving from *employee* (and boss's son) to *owner* and, more importantly, from owner to *entrepreneur* is the task before you.

Or, maybe you were working for a large home care franchise business and the branch you now own was more or less thrust upon you by a combination of obligation and opportunity. The transition from the Big Corporate environment to being a franchise owner to becoming a home care industry entrepreneur can bring a whole series of challenging phases.

Or, maybe you decided to invest in an established home care business on your own. Will it be a job or an asset?

These questions are not limited to home care but are relevant in all types of businesses:

- The auto mechanic opens his own tire service and discovers there is a significant difference between tire mounting and turnover.

- The college cafeteria baker opens her own bakery and learns the difference between meringue and marketing is huge.

- The band teacher at the local high school opens a musical instrument store. The difference between an intermezzo and inventory management is dramatic.

- The couple that loves to travel and stay in romantic bed and breakfast inns opens their own. The difference between romance and REVPAR (Revenue Per Available Room) is heartbreaking.

- The physical therapist opens her own home care agency and finds there is a huge difference between treatment plans and tracking payroll.

## The Job vs. The Business of The Job

The Job is not the same as *the business* of performing the Job.

All too often the new business owner takes the work he loves and turns it into a job, all the while thinking he is turning it into a business. This lapse in understanding crushes the spirits of so many that get into business with such high hopes.

The process is predictable. First is the thrill of new business ownership. Next, reality steps in. Then terror, followed by exhaustion and, ultimately, despair.

Why would this be? Because entrepreneurs do not go into business to get rich; they go into business to gain freedom, which never occurs when all you have is a Job.

And this Job is not even a good job. It is a job you cannot quit – your savings and credit are tied up in it. It is a job to which you cannot call in sick because there is no one else to do the job. It is a job you cannot sell to someone else – who wants to buy a job? It is a job that eats away at what family life you had, while you hope they understand you are "doing it for them."

When the final phase kicks in (despair), the business starts looking a little worn around the edges. There is no time or energy to make everything look perfect; there is no one to do the marketing when you are all tied up doing the management; the living breathing entity that was your business is a slightly tarnished, paint-peeled, smudged image of its former self.

## Getting Fired

So what do you do about it? If you are identifying with this, then keep reading. Before we are done we are going to "fire" you – and you will love it!

If you are not already in business, you are lucky. You get to start a living, breathing entity that may – or may not – hire you, but one that will have its own reason to live to reward you anyway.

So, once you are "fired" (stop working in the business as an employee), then what? The steps are laid out in the pages that follow but, suffice it to say, regardless of what job you think you are doing today, you are going to become a marketer – along with everyone else on your payroll, by the way.

As Dan Kennedy said in his book, *No B.S. Business Success*, "Nobody gets rich dusting shelves, changing light bulbs, keeping books or managing employees. ... The place for you to direct your time, energy, creativity, common sense, hard work and resources is marketing." (In Chapter 16 you will learn that *everything* is marketing.)

Getting you out of *The Job* is The Objective.

# CHAPTER 4

# Are You the Doer, the Overseer or the Entrepreneur?

Every owner of a business has an approach to the business that is derived from his or her core personality. This personality is developed early in life and is essentially hardwired into the psyche of the individual.

As I describe the three distinct types of business owner personalities, you will recognize people you know, including yourself – and maybe even the mentors who taught you the business.

The challenge for most people will be "rewiring" their programming to accomplish The Objective. Very few people are born entrepreneurs. Every business owner has the ability to be an entrepreneur; it is just harder for some than it is for others. Many will give up before they get there.

## The Three Faces

First, there is the **Doer**. This is the guy with The *Job*. This is the guy who gets things done. He has to, because the only one on whom he can rely is himself. Getting things done is his source of happiness, fulfillment and meaning. He wants to be the boss but he certainly does not want to have one. That is why he owns his own business.

Then there is the **Overseer**. This is the guy who has outgrown The Job and now has a business to run. Now _that_ is The Job! But it is different than the "Doer" because the "Overseer" organizes processes and cleans up messes. He perceives himself to be the boss and barely tolerates the idea of having one. That is why he owns his own business.

If "Overseer" does not fit comfortably in your consciousness, you may mentally convert the word to "Manager." The term "Overseer" was intentionally used instead of Manager because of the vague misuse of the term "manager" in common language. Using "Overseer" more graphically defines the behavior characteristics exhibited in this management style.

The third face is the **Entrepreneur**. This is the visionary. He needs Overseers (managers) and Doers in his operation, but cannot allow himself to be trapped into being either. He creates the systems for Overseers to execute and Doers to perform. He is the boss – unless he starts managing or doing. When he does, he stops being the Entrepreneur.

## Who's at The Top?

In all small businesses, there is one person at the top; the final decision-maker. In the description above and the discussion below, it is easy to slip into the idea that we are

talking about a hierarchy with three types of people in the same business, the entrepreneur a
t the top, the Overseers managing operations and the Doers doing the work.

To think this way would be missing the point. The fact is there are very few true entrepreneurs running businesses today. There are far more Overseers in charge – but remember, they also have the title of President. Over two-thirds of businesses are run by Doers who are also called the President. Therein lies the challenge.

## The Three Faces in Practice

Let's look at how these three faces manifest themselves in real life in more detail:

## Vision

The **Entrepreneur** creates a picture of what the business should look like at some point in the future and sets about changing the business to make it match that picture.

The **Overseer** runs the business he has and repairs damage when it occurs, while steadily moving it forward. His vision of the future extends as far as the next payroll, monthly report or quarterly summary.

The **Doer** does not think in future terms. He is committed to keeping things exactly the way they are today. His vision is right in front of him.

## Operational Processes

The **Entrepreneur** creates them. They are part of his system. They are the gears in his machine.

The **Overseer** organizes them. He does not always see them as part of a whole but he uses them to get things done.

The **Doer** plays with them. If one thing does not work, he tries another. There is no real consistency to them and one crisis creates a new operational process until something else happens so he can adjust it or create a new one.

## Opportunities

The **Entrepreneur** finds them or invents them. They are his main source of entertainment. They are his constant companions.

The **Overseer** sees opportunities differently. They are problems for him. They mess up his comfortable world. They represent more things for him to manage. This cannot be good.

The **Doer** greets opportunities with suspicion. They are overwhelming for a person who is far too busy doing what he is doing now. Opportunities are distracting.

**CHANGE**

It is the **Entrepreneur** who expects change. He relishes it because change creates more opportunities. It is the fodder for his imagination. Change is a wonderful thing to an entrepreneur.

The **Overseer** sees change much like he sees opportunities. Change creates havoc in the way "things are done." Change should wait until he is ready to accommodate it.

For the **Doer** change simply is not possible. He is far too busy doing what has to be done now to accommodate anything new. He will ignore it.

## Thinking

The **Entrepreneur** is always thinking. It is his Job. Thinking creates the vision from which all opportunities spring. Thinking is why an entrepreneur gets out of bed in the morning.

The **Overseer** is a little more pragmatic. This thinking thing is OK, but only about the current operation; the things for which he has responsibility. He does not want to think outside of these self-imposed boundaries.

The **Doer** would prefer not to think. Thinking is not work and there is always work to do. He knows what to do and how to do it. Why think about anything else?

## Profits

The **Entrepreneur** creates a machine that produces profits that will attract a future buyer of the business.

The **Overseer** directs a machine that produces profits that make him proud.

The **Doer** works to produce money to live on.

## Innovation

Innovation is the lifeblood of the **Entrepreneur**. If he does not create it, he finds people with whom to associate who can. It is the raw material for his entire world.

The **Overseer** is OK with innovation as long as it fits. If it makes his current activities easier or better, bring it on. If it changes the course of what he is doing, innovation is a little more problematic.

The **Doer** is not a fan of innovation. Doing things is what moves the world forward, not thinking up new things. There is too much to do to be innovating new things.

## Disruption

The **Entrepreneur** loves disruption. It is his sport. He makes the messes.

The **Overseer** puts up with disruption. It gives him purpose. He cleans up the messes.

The **Doer** hates disruption. He can only focus on one thing at a time. He avoids the messes as much as possible – but often lives in one.

## Parts of The Whole

The **Entrepreneur** sees his business in the entirety and drills down to the parts.

The **Overseer** sees the parts of the business as the spokes of a wheel with him in the middle.

The **Doer** has all these parts which he mentally collects as the whole but, which he can, generally, only work on one at a time.

## Control

The **Entrepreneur** is seriously into control. He creates systems to establish control in his business world. Control allows him the freedom to think, innovate and disrupt.

The **Overseer** maintains order. If he is in a team with an entrepreneur, his order comes from the entrepreneur's control. On his own, he is not in control beyond what he can manage himself.

The **Doer** does not worry about control. He is doing it all himself anyway. There is nothing to control except himself. His world is limited to that which he is doing. There is always plenty to do.

## Tense

The **Entrepreneur** lives in the Future tense. Everything is an opportunity. Everything is focused on Tomorrow.

The **Overseer** lives in the Past tense. What he does today is determined by what he did in the past. He is focused on Yesterday.

The **Doer** mostly lives in the Present tense. Everything he thinks about is right in front of him -- Today.

## Psychology

The **Entrepreneur** is the dreamer. Anything is possible.

The **Overseer** is wary. Anything can happen.

The **Doer** is the worrier. Anything can be trouble.

Perhaps you recognize yourself as one of these three "faces." Clearly the majority of business owners today are Doers. A sizable number, perhaps 25 percent, are Overseers. Relatively few, somewhere in the range of five percent, are Entrepreneurs.

There is no expectation that a Doer will wake up an Entrepreneur – even if he reads this book three times. There is the absolute probability that the Doer or Overseer will find him or herself dramatically changing the way they do or manage things if they have a clear understanding of what an Entrepreneur is. Picking up a dozen tips and shifting their strategies accordingly will move any business owner much closer to The Objective of freeing him or herself from the daily grind and growing the business to a point where it is less dependent on the owner to make things run.

As you review the descriptions of the Three Faces above you will see a pattern. The Entrepreneur takes an expansive and inclusive view of the business. The Overseer runs the business with not much view of the past or future, all the while keeping the train on the track. The Doer simply does. And does. And does. Anything other than the task at hand is a distraction.

The Entrepreneur integrates the elements of the business into his vision. The Overseer manages the elements for which he is responsible. The Doer sees the elements as his job to get done.

Your business will be in constant chaos without a true vision and plan for growth and profitability. If you do not already have that "entrepreneurial gene," at first it will be uncomfortable to separate yourself, "the nurse" from yourself, "the business owner." However, only when you can see your business as an independent entity can you ever hope to be free from the daily responsibility of running it. Only then will the freedom that all business owners seek be possible. It is The Objective.

# SECTION TWO: Clearing a Path

## CHAPTER 5

# Is It Really a Risk?

"The real objective of an entrepreneur is to *manage* risk, not *take* risk."

-- Dan Kennedy

Quite often when asked to define the term entrepreneur, people will include the word *risk* with their definition. *Risk taker, Risk Manger, Willing to take risks.*

In this chapter we will set aside the "Three Faces" definition for a minute and resolve to define every business start-up as an entrepreneurial enterprise regardless of the status of the owner in the *Entrepreneur / Overseer / Doer* trilogy.

The late quintessential entrepreneur, Wilson Harrell (*For Entrepreneurs Only*), made the shocking declaration that entrepreneurs never take risks. "The entrepreneur who knowingly takes risks," Harrell stated, "is a fool."

The entrepreneur never takes a risk because he or she, of all the people in the world, is sure that the idea will work. Absolute conviction! Cannot lose! Sure thing!

Harrell goes on to point out that the entrepreneur's wife may think he is taking a risk. The entrepreneur's banker will see the risks. The entrepreneur's friends, relatives, former fellow co-workers and suppliers will see the risks. But not the entrepreneur.

Such confidence is essential for any business to ever get started. Rarely does anyone start a business to "try it out to see if it works." Because he has analyzed the challenge and built a plan, the entrepreneur does not see himself taking risks.

## Self-Confidence vs. Blind Optimism

While the entrepreneur tends not to see the risks, there is no assumption that he is a fool either. The danger in blind optimism is that, of course, you could be wrong.

You see it every day. The corner location where "nothing goes" is the new home to an ethnic grocery with a limited population from which to draw. In your head, you say, "I wonder how long…"

Self-confidence, on the other hand, is vital to the prospect of the business getting off the ground. Without the dream, and the confidence that the dream can be achieved, no business gets started.

Blind optimism, on the other hand, is misplaced self-confidence. It is confidence without foundation. So what is the difference?

## Optimism + Information = Confidence

Take optimism and add information to create confidence. To have confidence, however, you must have adequate information. That is where research comes in.

**RESEARCH**
This chapter is devoted to the concept of risk and research. Research minimizes risk; it makes risk manageable; it reduces risk. It reliably shifts optimism to confidence.

Referencing Wilson Harrell again, he coached his small business clients to try the "Well, I'll be Damned" test. The test is amazingly easy and accurate. Take your new idea to 20 potential *buyers* – not family and friends, but people who could prospectively buy the product of your idea – show it to them and see how they react. If they do not say something reasonably close to "Well, I'll be damned!" or "Why didn't I think of that?" you may want to take a pass on your idea and try the next one. To change the world – and move you toward The Objective – your idea must have "Gee Whiz!" power with people in a position to write a check for it.

Dan Kennedy has a set of rules in his *No BS Guide to Business Success*. One of those rules is "Do NOT trust your own judgment."

## When to Conduct Research?

This could be a short section: *Every step along the way*. But there is more.

Of course, all business plans are based on research. To discover the opportunity, research is required. To describe a path where the business is headed, research is required. To get funding from any knowledgeable source (assume family money is excluded here) research is essential. So, of course, research is vital to getting started.

But this book, while helpful to prospective owners, is not generally directed at start-ups. There is not even a chapter called "Writing the Business Plan" because that topic is covered extensively in other literature. Chapter 8 suggests some adjustments to your existing business plan, but does not get you started from scratch.

As we were researching this book, Tim talked to many people in the Healthcare at Home business. Consensus in the industry is that relatively few people have formal, written business plans. If you are in that number, know you are in the majority and do not despair.

While this text may motivate you to start recording your plans, doing so may not be critical. What is critical is that you have a good understanding of what is going on outside your agency. Knowing trends, opportunities, threats, regulations and technologies as they may impact your business, is what is critical.

So, if research applies to start-ups, how does it apply to going businesses? *Every step along the way.*

The aware business owner is mostly cognizant of the fact that he or she does not know it all. The business owners, with greatest awareness, know that they do not know. Who could know it all? You say you have met them!? They generally do not stay around too long.

So, assuming you are interested in being around for a while, even growing the business to the point where it does not rely on you for daily survival, research is vital. In fact, the ultimate goal of any true entrepreneur is to establish the business to the point where he is free to do constant research – either to expand what he is doing now or discover what to do next. The entrepreneur is always living in the future. The future is revealed through imagination -- and research.

## Research is an Ongoing Process

There is an endless supply of information flowing at every business person. Sometimes it is only necessary to step into that flow. Reviewing the "Three Faces" you may realize that the Doer has little chance of getting caught up in the flow of information because he or she is far too busy making a living in the business. Without him or her, business would simply stop.

**HINT:** The enlightened Doer *does* stop and close the business for a few days to do the research. The enlightened Overseer may let loose of the reins for a few days to do the same thing. Unfortunately, it is all too rare. And, thus, the cycle continues for the Doer and the Overseer.

The Entrepreneur seeks sources of information that are not always immediately in his path. He is always looking for new facts, a new relationship, a new source, a new Oracle. Where do they look? Here are a few examples:

## The Morning Newspaper

The first research of the morning is often in the front yard when you wake up. The aware entrepreneur is always alert for new developments, trends or events. Those closest to home are the easiest ones to which the aware entrepreneur can react.

The morning paper may announce a community event in which the owner can be involved and, thus, gain exposure; it might tell of local, state or national legislation that could dramatically impact a home care agency. Skim it if you must, but do so daily.

## A National Newspaper

Newspapers that focus more globally such as the *Wall Street Journal*, the *International Tribune*, *Investors' Business Daily* or *USA Today* offer information about new trends or upcoming events. The aware entrepreneur will use these as regular resources of research.

## Supplier Salespeople

Those who work for your suppliers and call on others who are in your business, or related businesses, will have knowledge that they may be eager to share. Treating suppliers as teachers rather than *vendors* will pay off generously in terms of information. There is the side benefit of better service and maybe better terms when you demonstrate your respect for their knowledge. While you would never expect an ethical salesperson to share confidential information with you – and you can destroy them as a source if you ask them to – there is lots of information that is not confidential. This is information you would never get as quickly as you would in a respectful relationship with those who provide you with supplies and services.

So the next salesperson who shows up in your office should be offered a chair and a cup of coffee. Develop that friendship that goes beyond buyer-seller. Casually, but purposefully, pick his brain for ideas, news, gossip and trends. He is not a salesman; he is a news source, maybe even a databank.

## Call Around

You or someone on your staff can call competitors' businesses and ask questions. You will be amazed at what information you can get just by asking a few questions.

## Call Your Own Business

Another source of great insight can come from pretending to be a prospective customer for your own business. Call the agency office and ask questions typical of a prospective client. You will get a life-sized view of what your potential customers are experiencing. If you are concerned about your voice being recognized, have someone else do it while you listen.

## Online Search

There are hundreds of search engines available but, for our purposes, we will convert the noun "Google" into a verb. Google yourself. Google your business. Google competitors. Then Google everyone you can think of in your industry even if they are not local. Do not start with any particular information goal, just do the searches. This scavenger hunt can pay off dividends that will surprise you. Clip and save whatever you find that might pay off in the future. The good news is that doing the same searches 30 days from now will reveal new and different results. Change is constant.

Notice, too, who shows up in a local *Google* search. Do you? Make sure you have claimed your Google listing. It is absolutely free and absolutely necessary. Do it today, if you have not already. Where do you rank? Who ranks above you? Can you figure out why? How many reviews do you have? Does your claimed listing offer all the information Google allows you to display? There is a lot more information about this topic in Chapter 17.

## Trade Associations

State and national associations are the best sources of timely education through publications, periodic seminars and webinars and annual conventions. In general, they are assets to every Healthcare at Home business. Unfortunately, today, there is no one national association that meets the needs of every type of agency, so multiple national memberships, in addition to your state association, though expensive, may be necessary.

Though the lines between the lanes are dotted rather than solid, national associations tend to serve the interests of either Medicare-certified for-profit agencies, Medicare-certified not-for-profit agencies, private duty agencies, hospices, home infusion specialty agencies, and home medical equipment providers. Tim Rowan keeps a current list of links to national agencies on his web site at **http://homecaretechreport.com/resources**.

More than any other single thing you can do, attending industry meetings provides you with the opportunity to meet people in your business that are almost always willing to share ideas, and suppliers who have new and different products and services about which you may not be aware. As above, when we discussed supplier salespeople, if you go into a trade exhibit with the idea that every booth contains a teacher rather than a salesperson, your entire experience of the exhibit will change.

## Directories

One additional benefit to national associations is that you gain access to membership directories where you can locate colleagues you have never met, but who may be willing to talk, share ideas or collaborate in non-competitive markets.

## Networking

Attending national conferences and state association annual meetings is like free money. Approached correctly, it would be difficult *not* to get your investment back many times. Attend as many as you can afford, favoring the ones with the best combination of relevant presentation topics by the best speakers, and good attendance by both your peers and exhibit hall vendors.

## Government Publications

The U.S. Government spends millions of dollars conducting statistical research on every manner of business. While these statistics are broad and general, they can often reveal trends, if you know what you are looking for. Generally, you will be on a research path that defines what you are looking for before you go to secondary data such as that provided by government sources. Still, do not overlook it. You will find printed government statistics in most large city or university libraries. Much government data is online as well.

Although not a Government Agency, the *Encyclopedia of Business* consolidates many government numbers and interesting background information free online.

## TRADE PUBLICATIONS

In addition to Healthcare at Home: The *Rowan Technology Report* (**http://homecaretechreport.com**), published by one of the authors of this book, there are a number of print and online resources that should be on your subscription list. State and national associations have their own newsletters or magazines but some of the best information often comes from independent sources.

Some associations, and some independent publishers, support online discussion groups in the form of listservs. These are other good ways to consult with your peers but, keep in mind that answers you may find in thee forums are opinions and anecdotes, not data upon which you should make important business decisions. Just because a process or a product served one business well does not mean it is right for yours.

## General Healthcare or Other Business Magazines

Ideas come from many sources. The publication does not have to specifically relate to healthcare to be of benefit to you. Often the best ideas come from a parallel universe. Something common in one business may have not yet been considered by another. And, since growth is the core of entrepreneurism, that growth can come just as easily from adaptation as it can from innovation. Magazines devoted to small business like *Inc., Entrepreneur* or *Success* will usually be more relevant to the entrepreneurial enterprise than business magazines devoted to the global business picture like *Business Week*, or the *Wall Street Journal*. Just because they have a more global view, however, they should not be ignored. Ideas can come from anywhere.

## Books

Well, you are reading this one, so what is there to say? General business books or any non-fiction book that deals with issues that expand your horizon can be fodder for the imagination and should be included in the daily diet of research for your business.

While there are few books written specifically for the business of in-home care, one industry veteran has produced several, all of which are helpful to both newcomers and longtime agency owners. Tina M. Marrelli, MSN, MA, RN, FAAN, is the author of the *Handbook of Home Health*

*Standards: Quality, Documentation and Reimbursement,* which is in its fifth revised reprint edition. Targeted topical books include *The Hospice and Palliative Care Handbook* and the best-selling home health aide educational system *Home Health Aide Guidelines for Care: A Handbook for Care Giving at Home* and its accompanying Nurse Instructor Manual. Ms. Marrelli served on the workgroups that defined the first hospice nurse standards and also served as a reviewer in 2014 for the revised *Home Health Nursing: Scope and Standards of Practice* published by the American Nurses Association. She also worked at Medicare's central office (Centers for Medicare & Medicaid Services or CMS) for four years on Medicare Part A home care and hospice policies and operations, as well as serving as the Interim Branch Chief for Medicare Part B. She served for eight years as the editor of the peer-reviewed journal Home Healthcare Nurse (now Home Healthcare Now).

Her newest books, *Handbook of Home Health Care Administration: Sixth Edition* and *Home Care Nursing: Surviving in an Ever-Changing Care Environment*, are excellent places to start familiarizing yourself with Healthcare at Home's historical and current issues.

Another author you should add to your library is Marilyn Harris. Often referred to as "the Bible" of the industry, *Handbook of Home Health Care Administration*, edited by Marilyn Harris, MSN, RN, CNAA, BC, FAAN, is now in its sixth edition. Ms. Harris has been a home care nurse almost since the home health benefit was first defined in the law that created Medicare. Her handbook assembles dozens of the industry's top experts to write peer-reviewed articles on topics ranging from clinical to financial to technology to marketing.

## Internal Documents

Much can be learned in your own organization. Look for trends in buying patterns, the evolution of employee benefits, utilization of contract staff and the like that may have shifted over the years as the business grew (or shrank). Useful data can be found in old Medicare cost reports, employee manuals and printed reports generated by your computer system.

Risk is modified by knowledge. The majority of this information is absolutely free. The enlightened entrepreneur knows that he does not know it all. All too often the small business person thinks she already knows it all – or is too busy working in the business to find out.

# CHAPTER 6

# Nobody Really Understands

Spouse, children, friends, neighbors and employees. All of them are rooting for you to succeed, aren't they? In fact, if you make a list, you are likely to discover that there are dozens of people pulling for you. Or are they?

Building a business requires massive numbers of hours in the early days. There is always the danger that people with whom you have the best relationships will grow jealous of the time you spend achieving The Objective and start pulling against you instead of with you.

They say few marriages survive law school or medical school but entrepreneurship runs a close third. Sometimes these are just petty jealousies but often they are genuine concerns. Rarely obvious, the business owner often must be trained to look for them. This chapter will serve as your hunting guide.

You have heard it so often you are tired of it but we must say it. Most people who start businesses fail. Nevertheless, thousands of businesses open their doors every year. Perhaps it is human nature. Most people who go to Las Vegas also lose, yet planeloads of them arrive every day. Why do these people do this when the odds are so stacked against them?

Frankly, if it were easy, anybody could do it. Because it is not easy, it takes not just anybody but a special person to make a business successful. What we are trying to impress upon you is that it takes an entrepreneur to make a business successful without the daily, hands-on involvement of the person who started it. Whether or not you qualify under our definition of an entrepreneur, thinking like an entrepreneur can make a significant difference in the success of any project.

## It's A Lonely Job

Entrepreneurs are lonely. The most successful ones, anyway. They often find themselves torn between the business and the most important people in their lives; people from whom they must sometimes create separation just to get the job done.

This may be employees who want more but do not bring a full effort to the table. It may be a spouse who creates some sort of an emotional balance scale that "proves" you love the business more than you love him or her. Occasionally it is friends who teasingly call you a workaholic as they leave the pressures of their job at 5:00 in the afternoon. You begin to feel as though nobody really understands.

This chapter will make you feel better.

## Entrepreneurial Insanity

Entrepreneurs are generally intelligent people who should know how they are viewed by employees, spouses and friends. When that view is not what they would like it to be, they may pretend to laugh it off but, are they only laughing on the outside?

Entrepreneurs are lonely, almost by definition. Rarely does anyone else fully understand the passion they feel for their success. One source of entrepreneurial insanity comes from trying to please everyone, which guarantees pleasing no one – including the entrepreneur.

The irony of it is that the entrepreneur, at some level, believes what he or she is doing will benefit each of those people in his life – someday. How is it, the entrepreneur wonders, they never seem to understand that?

The entrepreneur genuinely wants employees to earn more and to gradually take on more responsibility and gain more autonomy. In exchange, they need to buy into the vision and contribute to the success with almost blind loyalty.

The entrepreneur genuinely wants his spouse to share the fruits of his labor; to celebrate together when the job is "finished" and the freedom to travel and play finally arrives. To get there the spouse must have the patience of a saint and the faith that the day will actually arrive.

The entrepreneur genuinely wants to go home at 5:00 like the friends who tease him about being a workaholic do. He longs for those Saturday barbeques and football Sundays he used to have when he was someone else's employee. Those things will return but only after the business is "ready."

Success requires emotional independence before the entrepreneur can enjoy financial independence.

Sadly, employees, spouses and friends are not always as patient as the entrepreneur. All too often, it is those most significant relationships that become the entrepreneur's most significant *anti-success forces*.

Even more sadly, the committed entrepreneur must take steps to protect him or herself from negative forces, even when they come from loved ones. That may sometimes mean different employees, new friends and, in the absence of saintly patience, the loss of a spouse.

Let's look at each of these important influences:

## Spouses

Do not misunderstand this message. It is not our recommendation to the reader that success requires, or causes, divorce. It is a statistical fact, however, that the rate of divorce among entrepreneurs is higher than that of the average population. Limited money and loss of personal time, particularly when both used to be more plentiful, are great incendiaries for matrimonial discontent. If you are an entrepreneur, you may be able to prepare your lifemate in advance of starting the business. Your specific strategy is beyond the scope of this book and the expertise of its authors but there are any number of resources out there, by both professional and pop psychology authors, to help you.

If you are already engaged in starting or growing a business, your spouse already knows who you are and what you are all about (but, still may not understand). Occasional reminders are important, as are occasional days off, as long as you do not cancel one at the last minute for a business "emergency." Be careful what you promise.

If you are the spouse of the entrepreneur it may be helpful to remember that he or she does not love you less than the business. The business is a different passion, not necessarily a competing one, though it does often compete for your time and attention. If you can join the dream rather than grow jealous of it, even if you do not join the company (usually a bad idea anyway), your marriage will outlast the formative years of the business into a rich, full life.

The only reason that the odds are against this is there are few couples with the tools to talk it out sufficiently to make it work. Those who do are rewarded multi-fold.

To pull this off, you must have established a clear statement of your goal, which returns us to: Define The Objective. At least you and your spouse will know what you are talking about, get an idea of what it will "cost" to get there (we are not talking money here) and will recognize when you are succeeding. Revisiting The Objective from time to time, especially when things get rough, is one possible way to regroup as a marital unit.

## Friends

Entrepreneurism is not for the thin-skinned. You will take your share of criticism from even those well-meaning friends who think you are insane to do what you are doing. More often than not, these sane friends are unhappily stuck in their own jobs and are secretly jealous of your freedom.

Good-natured ribbing may be okay in the short term but, when it starts to wear you down, when you begin to make decisions based on what others will think or say, it may be time to get some new friends. Time spent around negative, fearful, skeptical, doubtful people will sap your strength. Without strength, your resolve to achieve The Objective is damaged. Remain focused on the freedom in your future, the freedom your friends think you already have!

If you are thin-skinned and the negative comments of your well-meaning (or not so well-meaning) friends introduce doubts and begin to impact your decision making, it is time to get a "real job" and stop pretending to be an entrepreneur. You will be miserable otherwise.

There will always be those around you who are loyal to your dreams and support you when you need it. These people are gifts from the Universe. You must keep them close so they can nurture you – and you, them.

The move away from negative people does not have to be as dramatic as slamming a door. You simply choose to spend the time you have with different people – people who either "get it" or support you even though they do not. Do this for yourself out of respect for your resolve to achieve The Objective.

Believe it or not, you are likely to find that you do not even need to seek out new friends. They will find you! And it will happen through some sort of natural process. When you make the **Declarative Statement**, it happens faster. More on that at the end of this chapter.

## Employees

These can be the easiest and the hardest of your *anti-success forces* with which to deal. They are the easiest because you are buying their time for a fee and can simply stop buying it. (Few business people think about employees as fee-for-service, but it is far healthier for the business when you do.) When they are not a profitable investment, you simply stop buying their services.

It is harder when these same employees are the ones who were with you when you put the first dollar into the cash drawer. They are your pioneers, often your friends but, make no mistake about it, they are not your partners. If the place goes down, they lose a job; you lose your life savings.

There have been many articles written about employees who "manage the boss" through subtle and insidious blackmail. In the business of providing in-home care services, this takes the form of a unique scenario.

As this is written, a nursing shortage has been in place in the U.S. for years. Recruiting quality clinical staff is a nearly daily obligation for every agency owner, even if the task is delegated to the agency's Director of Nursing. Consequently, open RN and LPN positions are often filled by the "next available nurse," not by the "best nurse available."

The law of supply and demand means that this presents a dilemma. Underperforming employees that place a drag on the business need to be replaced but, in such an environment, there is often no replacement available.

A nurse with inadequate clinical skills can damage patient outcomes, perhaps taking down with it patient satisfaction scores that may result in negative online reviews. A nurse with inadequate patient assessment or documentation skills can do even more damage. Documentation impacts payment levels, compliance with federal and state regulations, risk of payment denial, and risk of being accused of engaging in fraudulent practices. This brings with it the possibility that the entire agency could be barred from doing business with the payer making the accusation. Sometimes payments are suspended from the moment of the accusation, not months or years later when appeals have been exhausted and fraud is proven. This is especially true with public payers such as Medicare and Medicaid. In extreme cases, the business owner can be sent to prison.

Because of these conditions, under which every Healthcare at Home provider operates, nurses, and sometimes thera-pists, are disproportionately powerful. An agency may have a training program; it may even be a condition of employ-ment that every clinician participates in it. But knowing best practices and understanding compliance rules are not the same as following company practices and producing com-plete and compliant documentation.

Faced with a choice between firing a non-cooperative clini-cian who cannot be replaced – even if it means serving a smaller number of patients and living with less revenue for a time – and losing the entire business, the passionate entrepreneur must sometimes bite the bullet and let the uncooperative clinician go before too much damage is done.

"It's not personal," you tell yourself, "it's just business." Except it *is* personal. You invested in training that person, trusted him or her with the health and lives of perhaps hundreds of patients, and allowed yourself to think of him or her as a long-term pillar of your business.

You shake your head with confusion. While your objective was to achieve more personal freedom by hiring and nurturing them, it turns out *they had more freedom than you do!* It was the freedom to say, "I know what you want me to do but I am going to continue to do it my way."

There is nothing wrong with independent home health nurses. In fact, the ability to operate independently, miles from their nearest supervisor, is one of the reasons they can succeed outside the controlled hospital environment. Still, there is a way to keep them and grow with them, but never be held hostage by them. It gets down to *Systems.*

## Systems

Systems are independent of any one individual. You get to create them and you get to control them. Systems are what enable a company like McDonalds to experience turnover of over 200 percent a year and not miss a beat. They mandate a way every little thing is done – independently of who is doing it.

Michael Gerber stated it succinctly in the E-Myth, when he suggested the world is not generally populated with extraordinary people. Most employees are ordinary people. Successful businesses employ ordinary people using *extraordinary systems.*

Yes, McDonalds has an advantage you do not. There is an endless supply of people capable of pushing buttons on a cash register that calculates change for them. There is not anywhere near an endless supply of Registered Nurses. Therefore, to convince the entire staff you are serious, to convince everyone to follow your Systems, it may be necessary to make an example of one person. You will probably only have to do it once.

## Work or Play?

The thing that so few people understand about entrepreneurs is that they never see themselves as workaholics. Nor do their friends and family see themselves as jealous or resentful. Those friends see their own employment as a job. The entrepreneur sees work as play. It is the sport. And, as in any sport, a score is kept. For Doers and Overseers the score is usually dollars. For entrepreneurs, the score is more often kept by measuring the number of hours *not* running the business, but working on growing it, and eventually letting it run itself. The dollars just seem to happen.

## The Declarative Statement

The entrepreneur's Dream is his constant companion. Earl Nightingale said, "We become what we think about most." To create the Dream and hang on to it in the face of so many anti-success forces can be an act of courage. Some give it up, let it die. It is just too hard.

While the Dream is often quite private, there is another way to look at it – as a tool. See it as a tool that can quiet or at least quell the impact of most of the anti-success forces in your universe. To do this, you make A Declarative Statement.

Tell the world what you plan to do. Share the dream.

Sure, you will still have nay-sayers and detractors. But your Declarative Statement lets you spot them more easily. At least you know what they are nay-saying. All too often, the entrepreneur plays it so close to the vest, the detractors in their world do not even really know what they are detracting. They must come to some oblique assessment like, "you work too many hours," but have no idea what you are working on.

Once you make your Declarative Statement, you will be subject to scoffing by those who see you as you are, not as you will be. Ignore them. Do not allow them to cast you into self-doubt. After all, it is not their Dream, it is yours.

You will attract a larger number of supporters, including most – but not all – of your employees, when you have made a Declarative Statement. People who have something to contribute will be more willing to share, as long as they know where you are headed.

The process is very much like marketing research. Once you have stated clearly what you wish to accomplish, you will get feedback in ways you did not ever expect. Listen. But know that negative forces will be among the feedback you get. Use your filter carefully. Do not get dragged down by doubt when those who know less about your project than you do take shots at it.

Caveat: This does not mean you can close your ears to contrary ideas. Not all of those who disagree with you will do so with real or imagined malice. Constructive criticism can hasten your success.

One of the benefits of the Declarative Statement is that you will attract mentors who can truly help you too. Once you "put it out there," your Declarative Statement will attract all sorts of attention. You will grow as a result.

Listen.

# CHAPTER 7

# Entrepreneurial Terror; Think You're the Only One?

In the last chapter, we talked about the loneliness of being an entrepreneur. The business owner is the only one who is truly on the line when it gets right down to it, and this can be frightening.

Rarely does the home health aide who cares for your patients worry about whether her paycheck will be honored. The business owner is the one who lies awake nights worrying about that.

The Director of Nursing should not be worrying about whether the medical supply closet is stocked. The business owner is the one who frets over getting the supplier paid on time to ensure timely shipments.

No contract speech therapist concerns himself with overdue payroll taxes or state surveyors halting operations. The business owner is the only one who must deal with all these issues.

It is the business owner who makes commitments to investors and bankers. Only the *one in charge* will get the phone call when things go awry.

It all adds up to some potentially terrifying events, but that is part of the job. That is why achieving The Objective is so rewarding. All the above-mentioned nightmares are managed by the team you developed – and you enjoy the freedom and peace of mind that comes from knowing you trained them to handle problems exactly as you would if you were there.

Until you get to this point, however, there are going to be a few sleepless nights along the way. Sleepless nights springing from anger, resentment, grief, frustration, disappointment, depression, letdown and, of course, fear. You cannot be in the game without experiencing some or all of these emotions at one point or another. How much time you let them take from your focus distinguishes the farsighted entrepreneur from the short-sighted small business owner.

The challenge is exacerbated by the fact that often action (or inaction) does not show up in results for days, weeks or months in the future. By the time an auditor denies a claim, or a family contests an invoice, it is way too late to apply a "quick fix." Sometimes the delay leads to a surprise. Imagine the amazement of the pre-historic man when women produced babies! The nine-month distance between the action and the reaction was a total disconnect. Sometimes such disconnects occur due to the nature of the Healthcare at Home business too.

## Perspective

Earlier you were introduced to Wilson Harrell. Wilson has touched your life even if you did not ever see his name before you picked up this book. You know of, or have read Inc. magazine. Wilson was its publisher at one time. He touched your life if you have ever cleaned up with Formula 409. Wilson took a bankrupt cleaning solution provider and built it into a multi-million dollar enterprise before selling it to Clorox. You probably have never tried "Tosta-Pizza" because it flopped – Wilson created that too.

"Entrepreneurial Terror" is a term borrowed from Wilson Harrell; in fact, it is the title of the first chapter in his book *For Entrepreneurs Only* (Career Press, 1995). In that chapter Wilson writes, "Terror is something that entrepreneurs do not expect, cannot escape and have no way of preparing for. … Few people even talk about it. The truth is that those of us who have experienced entrepreneurial terror seldom admit to it. As a result, it remains a deep, dark secret. The terror is so secret, in fact, that each of us thinks he or she is the only one who's ever felt it."

In his many speeches, Wilson used a personal story to put business terror into perspective. His story is being retold here for that same purpose and to honor a man who meant so much to so many of us with his forthright, powerful statements of wisdom, lessons that he personally experienced before delivering them in his presentations.

Paraphrased here, Wilson tells of being shot down behind enemy lines in France during World War II. The French Underground prevented his capture in a unique way that makes the perception of terror all the more poignant. They carried his badly burned body into a corn field, dug a trench and placed Wilson in the trench. They stuck a hose in his mouth and buried him.

He tells of the darkness. He tells of the fear of Germans sticking bayonets down into the earth searching for him or shooting into the earth randomly. He tells of worrying someone would accidentally kick the hose – or if it would start to rain.

When it was safe, the French Samaritans would dig him up and feed him, then bury him again. For eleven days he "lived" like that.

And, lived he did, to the benefit of so many. We lost Wilson in 2004, but not before he taught us a little perspective about terror.

## Sources of Terror
**The terror of feeling that the whole thing is not real.** Leaving the comfort of an employed position can be terrifying, in and of itself. Starting a business from the

ground up puts the owner in a "starting from scratch" position with little stability or security. There is no history to go on and only a business plan for guidance (making the assumption there is one).

To begin with, working for yourself can be disorienting. There is no boss to tell you what to do. The days come and go, without a framework for measuring progress. It can seem like you are adrift.

Besides, by not having a boss, you have no support structure, benefits – or guaranteed paycheck. Scary stuff.

Some of this anxiety can be alleviated by having written goals on a daily, weekly and monthly basis, a framework against which you can measure progress. By achieving even elementary goals, a sense of "realness" sets in and soon confidence grows.

**The terror of failing your family.** Starting a business that you have convinced your dependents will be successful is a heavy responsibility, with plenty of "second-guessers" close at hand. This can be disconcerting, if not terrifying.

**The terror of Government Payers.** Aging demographics in the U.S., headlined by 76 million Baby Boomers signing up for Medicare at the dizzying rate of more than 10,000 per day for the foreseeable future, is terrifying enough. That the government insurance system for seniors, Medicare, depends on a trust fund that is running dry adds to the terror. The solution, recommended by the Medicare Payment Advisory Council and implemented by the Centers for Medicare and Medicaid Services, to slash payment rates and scour the industry for fraudulent or wasteful providers, is a source of system-wide terror of epic proportions.

The inevitable result of CMS's efforts to extend the life of the Medicare trust fund will be that a certain percentage of providers will be forced to close or be acquired. 2015 was the first year since 2000 that the total number of HHAs declined instead of increased. In 2016, the number was smaller again.

Some business owners, however, see this environment as an opportunity. When publicly-held companies and multi-state operations retrench to meet the expectations of payers, shareholders and lenders, sometimes opportunities open for the smaller, more agile company. This is the company that can make a decision at 4:00 on Monday and be taking action at 9:00 Tuesday morning.

This is why keeping a close eye on your competitive and community environment can dramatically improve your strategy and planning. If you have established a friendly relationship with a competitor, for example, you may be the first to know she is considering retirement, which may put you in a position to be the first to make an offer to acquire her business or hire her staff and absorb her patients.

It is legend that Bill Hewlett and David Packard started Hewlett-Packard during the depression. E-Bay, Google and Amazon emerged during the dot-com bust. A tough economy is a 'macro' event. Running a business is a series of micro-events. Micro-events are often only marginally impacted by macro issues when driven by companies who are agile, opportunistic and are not slowed down by having to support the burden of an existing infrastructure. Speed of action eases terror.

**The terror of loss of freedom.** Ironically, most people start their own businesses to achieve freedom. In fact, freedom is The Objective, when it is all said and done. Fear is introduced when the new business owner looks at the distance to be traveled between starting and achieving The Objective. There is lots of work to be done. Not having any time for yourself or your family can be challenging. It can be emotionally divisive. The business needs attention and your family needs attention. Which entity wins? Therein lies the source of an emotional struggle and the fear of that struggle can be debilitating.

Developing a business that involves your family can have good and bad results. Sure, it allows the family to be more engaged in the process. On the other hand, communication between family members tends to be "less formal" – and it can be difficult, if not impossible, to fire them when appropriate and necessary.

Being actively involved with other people who own their own businesses can be helpful. Even if you cannot discuss your particular business issues, the camaraderie of having others who are traveling your business-ownership path at the same time can provide support and perspective. There are any number of local business groups you can join. Do so. Sometimes these can produce strategic relationships too.

Additionally, being in a business that you truly enjoy can ameliorate some of the anxiety. If you love the business, the trade-offs and sacrifices are more easily accommodated.

**The terror of not keeping your head above water**. Cash flow. Start-up money can run thin before revenue can replace it. Operations, regardless of patient census, must be maintained. Growth requires capital. Not knowing whether cash flow will be sufficient creates fear.

The old expression, "Nothing happens until somebody sells something" is dramatically true. You may not consider yourself a salesperson but every owner is, until they hire a marketing manager, who hires a sales team, to handle that for you. Still, no one can sell with the same vision and passion as the founder. In your case, it is less selling than it is story-telling. You will always be the best salesperson for your company – even when it is not your "real" job.

Cash flow fear is resolved by sales. You are absolutely the shortest distance between the problem and the solution.

Never stop selling. Do not stop selling even when you have a whole staff of salespeople. Selling in this context does not necessarily mean cold calling. It means being "out there." It means telling your story. It means not hiding in the back office. It means being an active player in your community.

**The terror (and shame) of failing**. The humiliation of it! Your friends. Your family. Your former co-workers who watched you tell the boss to take that job and shove it! Failing in your own business is terrifying, not as much from the loss of cash as from your public failure to achieve the goal.

Nevertheless, 90 percent of new businesses do fail. With odds like that, perhaps there is another reason for terror. Interestingly, however, that number is much smaller (closer to 20 percent than 90 percent) for franchises – businesses built on the concept of systems.

Be reassured that most of the fear that you might fail originates from the "what-ifs" in your head, not from what actually happens. Most of those "what-ifs" do not occur, but they do sit out there and haunt you, like a boogey man in the dark.

Seen another way, however, failure is practically a require-ment for a truly successful entrepreneur. Some of the greatest names in business history have gone bankrupt at least once, including Henry Ford, J.C. Penney, Conrad

Hilton, H.J. Heinz, Frank Lloyd Wright, Walt Disney, P.T. Barnum, David Buick (cars), James Folger (coffee), Sam Walton, William Fox (movies) and Donald Trump.

A study from Tulane University's School of Business suggests that the average entrepreneur fails approximately four times before achieving significant success.

## Creating Your Own Buffer

Because entrepreneurs typically work in a sort of isolation, they often cannot acquire sufficient perspective. Self-defeating thinking can creep in when there is no one to help sweep it out. Compounded, it can make the business owner increasingly negative and doubtful. In a word, Terrified.

Keeping tabs on your successes is a good way to keep your terror under control. Small successes as well as large ones. The business owner does not always have someone there to provide the "atta-boys" that he got when working for someone else's company. It is one more thing on the list of items the true entrepreneur must learn to do, self-back-patting. No one else is likely to do it for you.

One other key thing to remember about the fear of failure is the difference between *business* failure and *personal* failure. Keeping the two separate is vital for the ability of the entrepreneur to get on to the next project. If it were easy, anybody could to it. Feeling guilt over a business failure is a wasted emotion. If your intentions were honorable throughout, prepare to move on. Remember the successful entrepreneurs who have done so – an average of four times each.

## The Burden

Perhaps as much as anything, entrepreneurial terror comes from the knowledge that ultimately there is only you. There is no one else who has ultimate responsibility for the end result. Larger companies enjoy layers of reports so there is always someone to blame. Or, decisions get made by committees so there is never anyone to blame. Sometimes large companies hire someone to blame just in case things go wrong; people who cannot get fired. They call them "consultants."

In businesses, there are lots of excuses but you do not get to use them. You generally do not get to tell anyone about the sick baby who kept you up all night or the unexpected state auditor who knocked on your door while you were across the country at a conference. You are not "saved" from blame by the frozen lock, power outage, flood-blocked streets, employees' personal issues, crashed hard drives, whatever. You own all of the excuses.

Before you get all glum about your sorry lot in the equation, understand that part of the Entrepreneurial Insanity process is to anticipate these situations and structure a plan or set of plans that mean that sick babies and icy conditions are not unfortunate surprises – they are expected! It is one more step toward The Objective – making your presence in the business insignificant to its daily operation. This is the cure for the Insanity.

That cure involves the development of a collection of systems to respond to every anticipated problem before it occurs. (Sick baby, frozen lock, power outage, blocked streets, employee issues, failed hard drives.)

Outside of terrorist attacks, there are very few new disasters. All disasters, anticipated or not, boil down to loss of personnel, utilities, funds or facilities. You can start inoculating yourself from terror by having a plan for all the disasters you can think up.

## Never Share Terror

Before this chapter closes, there is one more important thing to remember: never share terror! Do not try to share any of the terrors we have described with a friend. If he or she is not an entrepreneur, it is going to be like describing a roller coaster ride to someone who has never been on a roller coaster. They have no real ability to empathize with you so you will only sound as though you are trying to offload your fears to someone else. Good friends will tend to internalize your angst. Not fair. Strangers do not – and should not – care.

Even more important is to resist sharing your terror with your loved ones. If they are not working in the business with you, your terror can only make them despondent, or even sick. After all, you convinced them that this idea simply could not fail. If it does, they will learn soon enough. Besides, chances are very good that the situation that created your terror will be resolved before they find out. If it does and you have shared it, the only thing they will remember is the close call. Then they will be saddled with their own fear that it might happen again. It is better to keep your secret and see if your fears are justified.

Until then, understand that the terror you feel is just one part of the price for ultimate success.

Every entrepreneur experiences terror. Few talk about it.

## CHAPTER 8

# What Were You Thinking?

Owners of home care agencies start out with good hearts. Their inherent compassion drives their need to build a business that helps those who need care while providing an avenue to reasonable profit. The intrinsic goodness of that vision sometimes obscures the cold hard facts that their vision is still a business like any other.

As harsh as it may seem, a business is not fundamentally compassionate. Without proper planning and structure, it will die. Dead companies help no one and hurt many.

Unless you invested in your business out of personal savings or from trusting friends or family members, there is a pretty good chance you wrote a business plan. Bankers want to see them even if they do not believe them – and even if you have collateral to back up the loan. Sophisticated investors will not even talk to you without one. What's more, it is possible that, even if you did not need to raise capital to start your business, you were enlightened enough to prepare one just for yourself.

Even if you have never written a formal document, the questions often answered on a business plan that appear in this chapter will give you important things to think about.

Even if you did prepare a business plan at one time, odds are that it has not been updated since you wrote it. This is not always so with new business owners, but certainly it is in the vast majority of cases.

If that is your situation, this chapter should make you a little uncomfortable – at least to start. Uncomfortable because you will remember all of the things you said you would do that you have not quite gotten around to. The numbers you boldly forecasted make you wonder what you could have been thinking at the time. Do not sweat it. You have lots of company. Plus, there is good news.

Your business plan represented your best hopes at a point in time. You now have something real against which to compare it. Undertaking the rewriting of a business plan is not nearly as daunting as starting one from scratch. Further, if you have never written one at all, it is actually pretty easy once you are already running the business. There is a lot less guessing when you have experience, and your numbers will be a lot more realistic.

"But," you may ask, "why would I want to write a business plan, or even update an old one?" The answer goes less to planning than to thinking. Notice this chapter's title is "What Were You *Thinking*?" not "What Were You *Planning*?" Using the business plan as a framework simply focuses that thinking more easily. Besides, business plans have had a pretty standard format for years. Ever wonder why?

## A New Look at an Old Plan

In this chapter we are going to look at a few of the common components of typical business plans and restructure them into points of focus on current challenges you may be facing, specifically in home care. By reworking the key elements of a business in your head, you will come away with a clearer awareness of exactly what you need to do to achieve The Objective – less time actually running the business and more time focusing on growing it and having a life of your own.

**Typical Business Plan Question #1:**
*Describe your business and the products or services you plan to offer.*

Did you start out caring for seniors and add pediatrics? Have you added hospice to home health or Medicaid to Medicare? How does the answer to question #1 differ from the day you started? What have you learned in the interim that might have caused a shift, if any?

When you started, was it your plan to perhaps do all the OASIS assessments and assign routine visits to clinicians you would hire as your census demanded? Did you take a turn as weekend on-call nurse? How involved did you plan to be in the day-to-day operation of your business?

With some experience under your belt, you can now answer a question you were not yet able to answer when you wrote your initial business plan. Are you providing home care or are you in the *business* of providing home care? That is the question that guides you to the difference between the thinking of a *Doer* or *Overseer* versus an *Entrepreneur*.

As you rewrite this section of your business plan, focus on your role as the owner of a *business* that happens to provide care services rather than as a person who actually provides the services or who actively manages the process of providing patient services. It may not be possible for you to extricate yourself from the process right away but remember, this is a business plan not a contract. Plan what you want to do with your business – and your life – in this exercise.

*Doers do. Overseers manage. Entrepreneurs plan.*

**Typical Business Plan Question #2:**
*Who are the players in your company and what roles do they fill?*

Organization Charts are familiar to every business owner. Boxes and branches describing titles and reporting relationships lead up the trunk of the inverted tree to the source of all decisions and wisdom – you.

The challenge for every new and growing business is that there are more branches than bodies, more responsibilities than names to put in boxes. So they all end up in the same place -- your desk.

As a result, the formal organization chart usually does not even exist in small businesses. Why draw boxes when they all have your name in them anyway?

There is actually a good answer to that question and it gets down to systems thinking. You draw empty boxes in order to view your business when it is finished, not how it is now.

In the early days, the new business owner wears lots of hats, creating those 16-hour days and lots of missed school plays. To see the light at the end of this long tunnel, it is important to visualize the finished product. Face it. You are going to be doing many – if not all – of the jobs yourself anyway. Instead of running from task to task, picture a staff of five or six. If there is room, create their work locations and go there to execute their tasks. If your employees will not think you are crazy, buy six different color baseball hats and wear the designated color when working on a specific task.

The key is to remember that you are not doing one giant JOB. It is a series of distinct jobs that will soon be filled as resources allow and needs dictate.

## More Than Just Boxes

While the box and line map of your business is helpful, as you are preparing for growth, make sure that each box is "alive" with a purpose and an obligation. For each box, create a document that not only describes the job (the "job description"), but also outlines each job's duties and obligations.

When the jobs are more than boxes, it will be good for you to be able to imagine what the job is, what has to be accomplished by the job and how the success or failure of the job is measured. Then, when you are ready to employ someone to fill the box, you will already have a deep and thorough understanding of exactly what the job entails, whether or not the candidate seems to fit the responsibilities of the position and how the performance of the individual will be measured in the future. The new employee will too.

**Back to Exercise #2**. The purpose of this exercise is to plan how to replace your name with someone else's in all but the top box. For now, simply list the people on your payroll and the jobs they do. Make note of what percentage of their efforts require input from you.

If you have to tell them to do everything that you want done, you might feel important, even indispensable, in your role as the head honcho but this is a quick ticket to entrepreneurial insanity! You will be totally trapped in your important role and will have absolutely no freedom to do your own work (except after hours when everyone has gone home when you can get some quiet) or take a day off, or take a vacation, or some days, even be able to think!

As you rewrite this section of your plan, think hard about those who require the most and the least hand-holding. If you can remember, make a list of the last five questions each of them asked you. For each question, ask yourself if you had a "Policy" (system) to which the employee could have referred before the question was asked. Would you have had to be involved at all?

Next try to "price" each decision you made for the employee. How much would it have cost to have let the employee make that decision – *and be totally wrong*? Rarely are decisions totally wrong, but to prevent even a small percentage, most business owners will not allow that chance. This practice consumes them.

**NOTE:** Excluded from this experiment are questions that have compliance consequences with state and federal regulations, Medicare Administrative Contractors, labor laws and the like. The cost of those errors would fall outside of your risk limits.

What policies could you put in writing that would eliminate a high percentage of your involvement with the kinds of questions with which you deal daily?

It may not seem like much when you are running a single agency but, what would happen if you opened a second one, or a dozen? To whom would the employees go for answers? This is the key to a growth mentality. It is the difference between owning a business and owning an asset.

*Doers do. Overseers manage. Entrepreneurs guide.*

**Typical Business Plan Question #3:**
*Describe your industry, its current and future prospects and how your company will take advantage of these facts. Describe the legal and regulatory environment in which you operate, including shifting expectations about reimbursement. Describe your services along with the features and benefits they provide the patient and his or her family.*

Is Healthcare at Home, as a sector of the U.S. healthcare system, the same as it was when you started? What changes have occurred? Have your processes changed since you started?

In the last decade, healthcare has changed more than at any time since Medicare was created in 1965. There is no reason to think that the next decade will level off and let you catch your breath. In response to system-wide changes, your business has no doubt adapted, causing it to change dramatically since you started. Is your business plan obsolete?

Perhaps you had a Medicare certified HHA but decided to add hospice or create a private duty division in a move to diversify. Maybe you are in a state that turned over its Medicaid operation to Managed Care Organizations and you have had to re-evaluate all of your insurance contracts.

More likely you are pretty much what you were when you started. Most business owners tend to stick with what they know; that with which they feel safe. But that is a double-edged sword.

Without change there is stability but that is only true if nothing else around you changes! With change there is insecurity because everything around you is changing. Both of those statements assume you are a victim of the market-place; that you have no control over events and must live a defensive life. Doers and Overseers tend to operate in a defensive manner. Entrepreneurs take an offensive posture.

The entrepreneur creates a business that allows him to stick his head out of the business long enough to assess the direction of the wind, identify new opportunities and steer the ship in the most opportune direction.

For example, are there opportunities in behavioral health, non-medical care, Home IV services, Assisted Living Facilities, or the rapidly growing new field of addiction counseling? In other words, now that you have found your nook, what crannies are available? Allow your imagination to wander in the direction of possibilities, not limitations.

*Doers and Overseers play defense. Entrepreneurs play offense.*

**Typical Business Plan Question #4:**
*What is your growth strategy? How large is your market? Is there sufficient demand for your services that you do not have to compete by discounting? Where are your avenues for growth?*

Analyzing a market and strategizing your marketing are often two of the more difficult tasks for a start-up company. If the business plan is to be presented to others, it is critical to make it plausible. Over-exuberance can lead to doubt among those less engaged with your new ideas than you are. On the other hand, assuming you have been in business for a while, marketing strategy should be a good deal easier. You do not have to guess as much about the market size, trends and the status of competition.

Your review of this topic invites you to look at the subject with a different set of eyes than you did when you first wrote your plan. Back then, it is likely that your vision was narrow

94

and focused. There is nothing wrong with that in a start-up. Few people are capable of broad vision at this phase. It is likely that Sam Walton never dreamed of the scope of his eventual empire when he opened his first small store in Bentonville, Arkansas. Somewhere along the line, however, he discovered that his style of management could be duplicated. That was the turning point. He changed from Overseer to Entrepreneur.

Whether you can develop an enterprise the size of Walmart or not, the pattern is the same. You, like Sam was a few billion dollars ago, have been in the business awhile and the time has come to do something different that will help you achieve The Objective. As you look at your growth strategy, what are the possibilities?

Can you *duplicate* what you are doing in other locations? This is the most typical expansion model, but it may or may not be the most profitable path for you. If you do this, you will need to have your systems down pat.

Can you expand what you are doing and serve more types, more age groups, of patients? Does it make sense in today's environment to open a branch in an adjacent city? Or, should you be looking to acquire an existing agency and operate it as a branch? Would it make sense to join a franchise for better brand recognition? Or, become a franchisor to allow others to benefit from your experience – and systems.

Once you have far-flung satellites, you have less personal control over day-to-day operations. That makes the need for published policies and written systems critical. Growth without systems can be very expensive.

So far, we have considered starting and growing businesses. The need to rewrite your business plan may also arise from the decision to narrow what you are doing. Perhaps you want to focus on your most profitable business segment. For example, if you currently serve Medicaid and Medicare beneficiaries as well as Private-Pay clients, would shrinking pay rates from public payers make it sensible to concentrate your efforts on your private duty side and Managed Care Organizations?

*Doers and Overseers maintain. Entrepreneurs grow.*

Digging out that old business plan and looking at it with new eyes may clarify a bit of the insanity with which you are living as you keep the business going today. Viewed within the context of your new entrepreneurial mindset and thinking strategically, you are likely to see your business with a much larger potential than you thought it had before.

Over the years we have seen dozens of business plan software systems. If you do not have an existing plan and you think it might be a good time to put one together, we suggest a program created by Burke Franklin at Business Power Tools that is economical and very easy to use.

## CHAPTER 9

# What Would It Look Like if You Were "Finished?"

In the previous chapter, there were several references to the importance of systems to create the freedom needed by a business owner to have time to grow the business. In this chapter, we are going to delve deeply into an understanding of what it looks like when you achieve The Objective.

## The Mental Image of Success

To help you better understand the rationale behind having systems at all and why they are the absolute key to your achieving The Objective, let's do a little "out of body" experience.

Suppose you are outside of your business looking in. You have successfully put your business together and you are considering selling it and doing something else. You are describing it to a stranger – someone who could be a prospective buyer of your business. Properly prepared, you have the wisdom to say, "Let me show you how it works!" not "Let me show you what we sell" or "Let me show you what we do." You get to show something more meaningful to a prospective buyer – your *system* for making money.

You want to be able to do this because you cannot sell your business! The business is comprised of people (including you), buildings and computers, and perhaps national and state licenses and certifications that cannot be simply transferred.

The only thing you can sell is the system within which your agency operates and through which it has become successful. It is the value you have added that makes your business worth something. That value is your set of systems. Otherwise, anyone can buy computers and hire nurses and start the same business. Why would anyone need to buy it from you?

How about your network of referring physicians, hospitals and community health centers, you might ask, not to mention your patient list? Do they not have value? Of course they do – assuming you have a system of keeping them current and viable. When it is time to sell your business, the names in your sales people's database will be more valuable than the names of your patients. They tell the story of your business relationships, built up over the years through careful nurturing and backed up by the strength of your reputation for patient care quality.

It would take the prospective buyer years to recreate such a list. Once you decide to seek a buyer, take care to grow that list and solidify those relationships.

In any case, referral sources cannot be owned. If you have trained them that, as the owner, you are personally the key to their happiness and no one else is as good as you, in effect you have reduced the value of your business. Far better to train physicians and hospital discharge planners to trust your brand, your clinicians, your mission statement -- not you personally.

If your business is good enough to be attractive to someone else, you have done more than simply unlocking the door every day. You have created a value by building *something* that people are willing to pay for. Systematizing that *something* is where you – or any employee – become immaterial to the value of the business. The business has value in and of itself.

"But," you say, "I do not want to sell my business!" In that case, if you have it ready to sell and elect not to, you have essentially bought it yourself. Plus, you have put yourself in a position where you always have the option to sell it or keep it. Either way, at that moment, *it has a value.*

Most people say they do not want to sell their business when, in their hearts, *they know they mean they cannot sell it.* They know they have nothing to sell! If you cannot picture the business running without you, the value of your business is pretty limited.

## Imagine Trees and Cows and Track

Perhaps one of the most valuable images you can have comes from Tom Watson, former CEO of IBM, who suggested that to get an idea of what your objective is you only need to imagine what your business would look like when it is "finished." When all the parts are in place, it runs as smoothly as any business can run. That is when you are not "doing" or even "managing," but *owning* a finished business. For now, your task is to simply work every day toward achieving that image. (Perhaps "simply" is not the best description of the process, but it made for a smooth sentence, didn't it?)

Imagine you own an electric train set. You want to set up a realistic scene to frame the train set. This involves all manner of little railroad crossings, tiny buildings, miniature people and pets, perhaps a mountain or two, cows in the little field, some trestles, cars and trucks, and smoke coming from the steam engine. Add realistic looking grass and trees and you have your own little piece of the world captured on plywood in your basement.

There are thousands of steps to take after the railroad tracks are stapled down, so you labor on, knowing in your mind what it will look like when it is finished. Still, right now, it is a pile of little bags and boxes of parts and a catalog of where you can acquire more pieces and parts.

Your business is exactly like that. You have all the parts, or you know where you can get them. Now it is a matter of putting it together in such a manner that it does not consume your life, but provides the means for you to have a life independent of the business.

Just like your business, you know realistically you are never really "finished" because the *Model Railroader* magazine will arrive every month with new little doo-hickeys you can add to your layout. Nevertheless, standing here today, you can get a mental picture of what the finished layout will look like when you get to the point where you are satisfied. That is the mental exercise to which you are being invited.

## Dream Time

Imagine what your "finished" business looks like. How big is it? How many employees? How are they dressed? What does the building look like? What are the colors of the walls? Where do your nurses, therapists and aides park? What does your car look like parked among them? What are you doing on a daily basis? What new things have you added since you first started imagining this finished project? What is your average daily census? How are referrals generated? What did you learn at the last national or state association conference that you have mentally added?

In your imaging of this "finished" business, you are totally unencumbered. You do not have employees that are important but uncooperative. You do not have a lease that runs too long in a location that you have outgrown. You do not have accounting records that you have not looked at in weeks because you were too busy *running* the business and not *owning* the business. What freedom!

You may add hundreds of imagined topics to fit your business but, when you do, make notes of what your imagination showed you. This is not a business plan. It might be called a "dream plan."

The wonderful thing about this exercise is there is absolutely no way you can be wrong! There is no risk. No one to tell you it will not work. No commitments to anyone about precisely what you will and will not do. It is your dream, limited only by your imagination. Your private plan. Only yours! There are no limits!

It is especially important not to limit your thinking. You are reminded of the quote from Earl Nightingale earlier in this book, "We become what we think about most." Limiting your thinking will limit your results. If you think you have a patient census of 100, you probably will. If you envision ten locations with 300 patients each, perhaps "failure" will hold you to only five, but the growth from your current base will still be phenomenal.

At this point, however, it is important to keep this dream to yourself. Others, who are not in the same place you are, will challenge your dreams, poke holes in your ideas and bring doubts into your process. You do not need those "negative forces" right now. Later when you have firmed up your vision, make your Declarative Statement and let them take their shots.

The next concrete steps, of course, are to start writing your dreams down. Use a pencil; keep an eraser handy and use it often. Add to your page with passion and adjust it at a whim. Soon, hopefully, with help from this text, you will gain a great deal of comfort with the business you own – and what it will look like when it is finished. You will love how it feels when you do not have to actually be on the premises to make it work perfectly.

This is the very essence of making the shift from small business thinking to entrepreneurial thinking. It is the only way to stop the *insanity* with which most business owners live day to day. It is the objective of this text to help you achieve that.

# CHAPTER 10

# How Do You Eat an Elephant?

The answer to the riddle is, of course, "one bite at a time." But, before this starts us off on a string of stale elephant jokes, let's get right to the point of this chapter. The insurmountable (eating a whole elephant) suddenly becomes quite possible when broken down into the smallest elements of the process (one bite).

Dr. Kenneth Christian wrote a book, *Your Own Worst Enemy: Breaking the Habit of Adult Underachievement* (Reganbooks, HarperCollins) in which he examines the reasons behind why adults do not achieve their full potential. In it he describes a series of exercises one can undertake to accelerate the process of changing personal habits. We have borrowed one of the tasks that Ken describes and added some home care examples to make the point clear.

The process involves dividing the elephant into bite-sized pieces, not by merely hacking it up, but by breaking it down into logical and increasingly smaller components.

**The Goal.** This is your elephant. This is the whole thing; the objective of your process. It is the objective that appears overwhelming, even impossible, when stated as one action, i.e. "eat an elephant." (The elephant analogy is getting a little long in the tusk. Let's replace it with a more relevant massive task: "I want to be able to sell my business.")

This is The Goal, and it should resonate with the heart of every entrepreneur. Feel free as we proceed to insert your specifics. For you, The Goal could just as easily be, "I want to buy out a competitor" or "I want to grow my census by 400 percent." You get to pick the goal. For our purposes, we will focus on the process of making your business ready to sell. You can adapt it to your unique environment.

Wouldn't it be nice if you could simply put a sign out front and wait for people to come by and negotiate with you for the transfer of your business asset? Everyone knows this is generally not going to happen. And so, to be prepared to achieve it, we break the process down into increasingly smaller components.

Step-wise these components include:
**GOAL >**

     **PROJECTS >**

       **TASKS >**

         **ACTION STEPS >**

           **ACTIVITIES**

**Projects.** To prepare any business for sale, any number of things have to be done. Let us suggest a few that might be necessary to prepare a home care business for sale.

**Project 1:** Clean and Clear. Your IT department has a computer parts graveyard that they will never use again. Your marketing department has obsolete promotional materials. Your billing department has outdated manuals on shelves next to current ones. Your rented storage unit has many more than the required seven years of records. And your own office has stacks of unread trade magazines. Clearing your business to make it more visually (and psychologically) appealing is a project.

**Project 2:** Adjust Staffing. You have people you have kept on because, well, they have always been there and they are friends of family friends (or, worse, family!). You have energetic contributors to whom you have not delegated enough responsibility. And you have a couple of holes in staffing you have meant to fill. Project 2 is to right-size your staff. Clear up all of those staffing changes you have been meaning to do but have not gotten around to.

**Project 3:** Clean up Corporate Records. In closely held companies, when the owner and his or her spouse may hold all of the board seats, corporate decisions rarely take on the importance they do in a publicly traded company. If you are going to get through due-diligence, you will need to clean up those records to show a timeline of decisions made, borrowings approved and officers elected. It is not hard – as long as you can remember all of the decisions you made in the name of the corporation since your last minute update.

**Project 4:** Put Systems in Place. Systems. Those things that make the operation run when you are not there every minute of every day. Systems actually make it possible to sell a business, since it is not likely that you can sell yourself or your spouse. If you make lots of critical decisions on a daily basis, replacing yourself with systems will make your business salable.

There would certainly be more than four projects to prepare to tackle the *Goal* but, for this example, we will stop at four. The next step is to break *Projects* down into *Task*s. For the sake of brevity, we will only look at one Project for our example, but you can imagine the types of Tasks necessary for the others.

**Tasks.** Breaking Projects down into Tasks makes the process more manageable – though not yet "bite sized." Defining the Tasks necessary to accomplish the completion of the Project on the way toward The Goal is the next step. Note: Not all possible tasks will be included. Those listed below are simply examples.

**Task 1**: Identify all areas that need to be systematized. In a home care agency, this might include taking referrals, scheduling initial and subsequent visits, collecting overdue invoices (home care) or appealing payment denials (Medicare/Medicaid), advertising and promotions, ordering supplies, vendor relationships, dealing with worker's comp issues and insurance companies, filing taxes, remote worker safety and a myriad of other things.

At the management level, you might include systems for decision making, public image and corporate value systems. Task 1 is to define them for your own business.

**Task 2**: Assess systems that are in place now. Are they written down? Are they being followed flawlessly? Could they be duplicated in another operation in another location and be understandable?

**Task 3**: Fill the gaps. Where systems are ineffective, they need to be rewritten. Where there are no systems, they need to be created and documented. Where there are systems that are not being followed, retraining must be undertaken.

Again, there could be many more tasks in this effort, but the above will serve as examples of the process. Next, we break the Tasks down into smaller pieces.

**Action Steps**: These are the easily understood and actionable items that are the foundation of every Goal. These are the pieces that are nicely contained in a single concentrated effort that is measurable and can be confirmed as complete. For our example, we will only work with Task 1.

**Step 1**: Organization. Purchase a 3-inch ring binder with section tabs.

**Step 2**: Prepare a format for each system description. This will include the name of the system, the rationale for it, the "rules" to be followed, the measurement process and the manager responsible for it.

**Step 3**: Consult with those involved in the process to ascertain full information about what is being done, what gaps exist and how the system should be articulated.

**Step 4**: Write the System Statement in the format described in Step 2.

**Step 5**: Review the written system statement with responsible staff to determine their understanding of it. Note: They do not necessarily have to agree with it after your explanation of the new system, but they do have to comply with it. It is *your* vision and *your* company. Too much pushback and the subject will come up again when you get to Project 2 (adjusting staffing.)

**Step 6**: Distribute copies of the new policy to those involved and store a physical copy under the appropriate tab in the binder you established in Step 1.

In the above example, the Steps were fairly logical in their sequence. However, in some cases this will not be as clear, which calls for a further division of the "bites" into those you should eat first and those that should come later. You will probably want to rank them from the simpler to the more complex.

**Activities**. While the above example the Action Steps are fairly discrete, if you have a Step that is more complex, you can go to the fifth level of the breakdown, to the Activities level. These are the "bites" we have been working toward.

For example, we could break down Step 4 (all of the departments impacted) into the various areas we listed for Systems in Task 1. You could easily write a one-page system for handling time records in a few minutes even less if you have automated systems in place. If you have more time, you could write two or three more.

The point of this approach is that every Goal gets down to the smallest parts. Tackle what you can and eventually you will achieve the Goal. Planning down to the minute "bites," however, is essential to not only making progress, but to eventually accomplishing The Goal.

## CHAPTER 11

# What Should You Hire You to Do?

Presuming you own an agency now, the question of who owns whom is probably one you have had in one form or another over the time you have been "the boss." Do you own the business or does the business own you?

You may have started the business to gain freedom of choice over when and where you are working – free from the demands of people who understand less about what you are doing than you do but who, nevertheless, have the prerogative to tell you what to do and when. You ditched all of that so you could do what you want to do, the best way possible.

## Power Shift

As the owner, you can do whatever you want. That is until the day when you have the business fully staffed and the nurse supervisor on whom you rely, simply cannot make it in to work due to a family emergency. Now how much freedom do you have?

Or, payroll is coming up on Friday, and a key managed care company has not paid its bill as agreed and cash is a little short. Whose paycheck does not get cashed – or, sometimes, even written?

Or, the fall family vacation you have planned for months is scheduled for the exact time that a new earlier-than-expected snowstorm hits your area and your staff's ability to get to all of those who rely on your agency is severely compromised. Who stays home?

In these instances, and a hundred more, the business seems to have power over your personal preferences. If you did not own the business, chances are pretty good you got your day off, your paycheck and your vacation as scheduled.

As the owner of the business, however, you have traded one boss for a host of different ones like bankers, investors, doctors, clients, government entities and, even, at times, employees.

Do you know that you could face severe penalties if you were to treat even one employee the way you are treating yourself?

## Easy In; Not So Easy Out

Perhaps you have seen or heard commercials advertising services to help new business people incorporate or form a Limited Liability Corporation. The text of the ad runs something like this, "If you have ever dreamed of owning your own business, get it started right by forming your very own corporation!" They make it sound like getting legally formed is the same as answering the dream.

The logic of this is much like, "If you have ever dreamed of owning a home of your own, we have a hammer to sell you." The distance between a real business and the articles of incorporation are as far apart as owning a hammer and owning a home. It is nonsense.

The aforementioned radio ad suggests that getting into your own business is the achievement of your lifelong dream. Any experienced entrepreneur will tell you that the achievement occurs not when you open the doors, but when you have turned over the keys to the next owner; when you have built, and profitably sold, the business. It is a lot easier to get into the business than it is to get out of the business. But, getting out is always the entrepreneur's goal.

## Finishing the Job

Earlier we discussed beginning with the end in mind. Getting a good picture in your mind of what your business looks like when it is "finished." This chapter deals with all of the time in between starting and finishing. All too often agency owners are so totally consumed by starting the business (Doing) or operating the business (Overseeing) that he or she never achieves The Objective of owning a business that provides them their long-sought freedom. Millions of lives have been literally crushed by the weight of business ownership. Those who survive are rarely as happy as they pretend to look.

It does not have to be that way. By maintaining the mental self-image of owner rather than operator, you can ultimately achieve freedom. Start that plan today!

## How Can I Be the Problem? I'm The Boss!

It is unnatural, uncomfortable and counterintuitive. Why should the person who starts the business be the one the business most needs to be rid of? Yet, if you are truly successful as an agency *owner*, there will be a time when you will become the agency owner, not a key part of the management. As your business matures, you will find that your personal success will grow in opposite proportion to the extent to which your business is dependent on you. Your original objectives of wealth and freedom will start to be achieved. You will be closer to The Objective.

It will not happen automatically but it must be planned. The objective of this book, therefore, is to assist you in making that plan.

Part of the problem is that all too often the personality and soul of those who start a business are all tied up in the creation of the business. Their egos are tied up in the idea that they are indispensable to the successful execution of the business strategy they created. It is their source of personal importance.

As a consequence, every decision, big or small, must pass through their fingers. All of the key information is kept in their heads; no one can make a decision without checking with them; they can do every job in the place bathing to bookkeeping – and, as a result, will tend to meddle in things just to keep that sense of importance.

Of course, along with all of that responsibility comes all of the stress. With no one else competent to make a decision in the agency, all of the pressure comes down to the owner. They keep a cell phone – maybe two – near at hand 24 hours per day. They are indispensable and irreplaceable. They never take a sick day; they cannot afford to! That goes for days off or (God forbid!) a vacation! More than a few families have been destroyed by such "responsible" behavior.

## Highest and Best

What is the highest and best use of your time? Assuming, as we did above, that you can do everything, is it wise for you to do so? You can probably do scheduling, bookkeeping, inventory control, marketing, sales (yes, marketing and sales are different jobs!), hiring, firing, training, opening and closing, pitching in where needed and handling various government inquiries. But should you?

Trying to do all of them may do more harm to a business than if you did none of them. Somebody must do them and do them correctly. But the sooner you let go of most or all of them, the more successful your enterprise will be overall. You cannot abdicate responsibility, but starting to get rid of as many specific tasks as possible should begin immediately.

Almost always, the agency owner's main job needs to be "story telling."

## Your Story

Your story is how you convey the mission of your agency to all with whom you come into contact. Here are some examples:

**Personnel Management**. If your employees know "The Story," they have a chance to place their own behaviors and decisions into a context they understand and can make others understand too. They learn the Story from their first interview on.

**Marketing**. Your existence in your community or marketplace consists of The Story. Marketing is far different from selling. Sure it sets up selling, but marketing "The Story" postures your enterprise to be understood by the audiences that it fits.

**Sales**. If nothing happens until somebody sells something, then nothing gets sold until The Story gets told. Since you get to write The Story, it makes the business uniquely you, but it does not mean you must act out the story by yourself.

**Bookkeeping**. Accuracy of your paperwork reflects your company's professionalism. This is more important in home-care than most businesses. There are so many ways to end up not getting paid, those responsible for it absolutely must buy into this part of The Story.

**Ownership**. Those who have responsibility for telling The Story will have a greater respect for the process if they understand it in the owner's visionary context. It minimizes sloppy work.

## The Decision

There are many steps to removing yourself from your operation. The first is the decision to do so. It is the hardest because it is the most counterintuitive. Accomplish this objective and you are well on your way to achieving The Objective.

# CHAPTER 12

# What Does Your Business Look Like Without You?

Everyone pretty much understands systems. When you catch a flight, you understand a system which has dramatically changed over the past twenty years.

You log in online, shop for your destination, best price and right time; buy a ticket with a credit card, the issuer of which will receive a check from you to pay for it. On the appointed day, you will prove, with a government-issued ID, that you are, indeed, the person whose name is on the ticket; and you will check your luggage knowing it has an additional fee to be paid for transporting it, that it cannot exceed a certain weight and it cannot be locked with a lock not approved by the TSA. Then, you head for Security where you will remove your jacket and shoes and all metal from your person, pull your computer out of your carry-on, walk through a metal detector and reassemble yourself on the other side. Soon, you will experience the thrill of showing off that "hidden" piercing to an, up-to-that-moment, bored screener. Everybody knows his or her part and, except for the stubborn or stupid, everybody moves through it routinely.

The whole process does not require the airport manager, head of TSA or the airline station manager to be involved. It is a system.

Every element of your business can operate on a system. If you cannot visualize that, you will be limited to owning and operating a small business until you pass it on, burn out on it, or die. Chances are very slim that you can ever sell it for a profit – particularly if you include the salary you would have taken had you spent a similar number of hours employed by your business, even at minimum wage.

## Why Systems?

You must have systems because you simply cannot do everything yourself. Even if you delegate and tightly supervise, you cannot manage all the aspects of a business that is growing. There are a certain limited number of things that both interest you, and at which you excel. If anything, those are the things you should be doing. If you are growing your business fast, even those things you love doing will be systematized and performed by others.

Once you are operationally sound with reliable and predictable systems, you will systematize marketing and sales. You will not be able to personally visit with each referral source that could send business your way. You will take your special personality and "Story" and convey it to a team of people who will represent your company just as you would yourself. The process is logical and predictable. You only think you are the only one who can tell The Story. It is not true.

One other thing to consider is that you are not invincible. You probably do not take sick days when your employees might. You are willing to "play hurt" to keep the machine moving. But, statistically speaking, at some point you will be pulled to the sidelines. You will have no choice. Whether it is an accident, significant illness or airline strike while you are out of the country, you must plan for the day when you will simply not be able to be there. Statistics suggest that one out of three business owners will experience a loss-of-time incident sometime during their working careers. With adequate systems in place, your business will be just fine when you return.

What you may have to guard against is the feeling of disappointment if it is operating better than when you left. Some entrepreneurs simply cannot help themselves and unknowingly slow progress rather than help it by their "protective" presence.

## What Systems?

The answer to that question is difficult to answer in a way that can be applied equally across the board. However, using this example, you may be able to extrapolate to systems that will work for you.

A home care agency, whether Private Duty or Medicare certified, lives or dies by the ring of the phone. Advertising campaigns and sales efforts are all aimed at attracting patients, their families and their physicians to refer to your agency instead of the one down the street. When the phone rings what happens may well be the series of events that separates thriving agencies from mediocre ones. That series of events is a system that is put in place by you, the owner. If you have done it right, it runs just as well without your direct intervention, which is the purpose of a system.

**Step one**: Who answers the phone? Hiring the right receptionist is half the battle. In a business like yours, where customers do not walk in the front door and buy products off your shelves, the voice of your receptionist is the first "face" of your company. The last thing you need is for it to be the last. No matter how skilled your nurses and aides are, no matter how wonderful their bedside manner, they never see the patient whose daughter or doctor was turned off the first time they call you. Your first step is to hire a great personality and train him or her to give the same first impression that you would.

**Step two**: Triage with a smile. In your training, you are going to build a phone answering policy that resembles an emergency room triage procedure. When she realizes the call is from a potential patient rather than a co-worker or a salesperson, she immediately and gracefully begins to follow your established system, with the same bedside manner as your best clinician. This part is up to you but consider how you might react to the following phrases we have heard from various receptionists and decide which demonstrates the attitude you would like to present to the world:

*Yes, we are currently accepting new patients. Please tell me the patient's name and his or her age.*

*I am so glad you called. We have a lot of experience with people your mother's age.*

*Is the patient incontinent?*

*How can we make your life easier today?*

*First, let me ask about your payment arrangements. Do you have Medicare or private insurance, or will we be billing you directly?*

*Our nurses and aides are experienced with all types of needs. Let me ask you some questions about your loved one's age and condition so I can find just the right caregiver for you.*

Note: (Some call this "Step 2b.") You should call from your home phone from time to time to see how your receptionist is following your system. After a while, they follow the system faithfully if they know that any caller might be you.

**Step three**: Backup. Of course, you have a system in place that handles several calls arriving at once; more than one receptionist can handle. You will probably call it the "Friday afternoon system" and you will realize that it means multiple people need to learn the way you want your phones to be answered. This step usually includes the reminder "everyone here is in marketing."

**Step four**: Directing the call. Your system includes clear directives about where each call should go after the receptionist's friendly, caring greeting routine is finished. Medicare referrals must go to the RN on intake duty. Private duty referrals might go to a scheduler (who is equally hired and trained for personality and bedside manner). Complaints from current patients and clients or their families might go to a designated troubleshooter or nurse supervisor. Your system will include feedback to the referral source and everyone knowing exactly who is to deliver it. Knowing the system and always redirecting calls correctly can also make the difference between a long-term patient and a hang-up.

**Step five**: Keeping the customer your receptionist won. The final step of your intake system is, once again, the one that recognizes the adage "every employee is in marketing." Whether it is your scheduler speaking to a potential client's adult daughter or a nurse speaking to a hospital discharge planner, they must continue the attitude that says, "we are so glad you called; we are sure we offer the services you are looking for." This part of the system is another one you will write and put in place. You know best what language and processes work best in your marketing area.

## Systematize Everything

Whatever your variations are on this theme, the point is that systems make it possible for the business to run without your direct daily intervention, which is what makes your business valuable to a potential buyer. Virtually every aspect of any business can be systematized. Think of how many types of businesses are franchised or have multiple locations under one ownership. Assume the business owner can do a set of tasks perfectly. The process is no more challenging than writing down the exact steps to take. All too often, however, there may not even be a system operated by the owner. It could be that each time something is done; it is done on a whim depending on the mood of the individual.

This is a recipe for inconsistency, if not disaster. What happens when someone else has to follow in the leader's footsteps – and there are no footsteps?

Therefore, the process for establishing a business operated by systems would include the following:

- Create a list of absolutely everything that occurs in the life of the business on a daily, weekly or monthly basis. This can be as mundane as the procedure for logging into computer work stations and as specific as how often passwords must be changed. It should be excessively detailed. Who keeps a master list of passwords? Or, where is the sysadmin's password recorded so no databases are left inaccessible in the event someone resigns unexpectedly. Other systems will include privacy and security practices, such as opening the building in the morning and locking it at night.

- Once the list of activities and processes is complete, look for ways to merge them into categories. The HIPAA procedures could include times when server rooms must be locked and who has the key, for example.

- Take each process and establish a stepwise system for accomplishing it. Too much detail is not possible. Leave nothing to chance. Imagine that the system must run the business and you are totally absent. Imagine that you own 100 such businesses and each must execute precisely the same systems.

- Next, look for ways to internally generate responsibility. For example, you can establish systems that apply to employee behavior. If you have a system for covering patient shifts when a CNA or aide calls in sick, it might state clearly how supervisors, schedulers and family caregivers are to be notified. The scheduler in this system understands both overtime rules and estimated travel times within the geography of your service area. Each employee "owns" the job that must be accomplished. This prevents not only empowers them to make decisions but their problem from becoming yours.

- Write everything down into a multi-chapter Operations Manual. Pretend you have never worked in the business yourself and decide whether you would understand your own instructions. Then let a few employees give you an honest assessment too.

- Have someone read a section who has never done the described tasks before. See how he or she reacts to the system and whether the tasks can be executed flawlessly. Obviously, if the task requires technical training before it can be accomplished, you need to have a trained person review your system description.

Perhaps the best example of how this works is McDonalds. This is a business that is based on the assumption of over 200 percent annual turnover and where the team members are generally teenagers. The only possible way for McDonalds to have become a multi-billion-dollar company is for the systems to leave nothing to chance. A McDonald's manager's job is less about managing teenagers than overseeing a system to which they have become attuned. The *system* manages the teenagers.

## Systems Are Investments

We have discussed how Systems create assets. Having systems allows the business to be less dependent on you. The extent to which your presence in the business is insignificant is the distance you have come toward developing an asset. You cannot sell a business because you cannot sell people and you cannot sell yourself. You can sell a System.

You can sell a set of systems that you have personally developed to make your business special and successful. These systems are your asset. It allows you to use the wonderful expression, "Let me show you how it works!"

# CHAPTER 13

# Who is Stealing from You?

Sometimes people do not even know they are stealing from you. When they steal time – whether yours or theirs – it is cash wasted.

Tim Ferris wrote a book titled *The Four-Hour Work Week* in which he extolled the benefits of time control (not time management) and outsourcing. His point was that in any given day, the average business person gets only about 90 truly productive minutes. It was a shocking thing to read but, upon reflection, seems about right.

Throughout this text, you have been peppered with ideas about how to create systems that allow your business to run on autopilot. Similarly, but not identically, the thesis behind Ferris' book was dramatically reducing the amount of time you spend running your business. It is almost exactly the same thesis as *Entrepreneurial Insanity*. The key difference in our philosophies is that in the case of *The Four-Hour Work Week*, the objective is to reduce the amount of work you have to do to make a living. We are encouraging you to eliminate your importance to the organization so that the business has a greater value. Whatever the objectives, the strategies are very much the same.

Earlier we discussed letting employees make non-legal decisions up to a certain dollar amount without your approval. Not only do your clients get answers more quickly, your employees gain face and you do not get disturbed. The saved time allows you more time to increase the value of your business. In theory (and practice) it will cost you less for employees to make limited-value mistakes than what you can earn for your business by not dealing with the distraction yourself.

Other ways to avoid interruptions is to stop reading e-mail. Not altogether, but not every time the little "ding" in your e-mail account announces you have a new one. Turn it off! Decide to open e-mails only twice per day. Put an auto responder message on your email system announcing your new policy and let people who need a more immediate response know they can reach you by your "private cell number in the case of an emergency."

It might require a bit of training to help your colleagues understand the definition of an emergency, but it will eventually pay off. Here is an example of an autoresponder message to accomplish this:

**Hello,**
**In an effort to accomplish more than is normally possible for one person, I have restricted my handling of emails to twice a day – 11:00 AM and 4:00 PM Eastern Time. I will respond to your message at the next opportunity. If**

the subject of your email is urgent and requires an immediate response from me, please call my private number at 555-321-4321.

**Thank you in advance for your understanding.**

**Sincerely,**
**Anne the Agency Owner**

Similarly, your office voice mail can announce that you will not be picking up messages except for twice per day. The same cell phone emergency procedure can be used to avoid a possible disaster that would be created without your input. Eventually, you may be able to reduce these tasks to once per day or a couple of times per week. You will learn how few "emergencies" there really are. Remember that this is a recommendation for you, the owner. We are not recommending that your clinicians' patients and family caregivers use such a message. And, naturally, you will allow key staff to knock on your office door with urgent matters.

## Get to The Point

When you are reached by phone, put subtle pressure on your caller to get to his or her point quickly. By answering, "Oh, Hi, Jim. I am right in the middle of something but, tell me what I can do to help you." Jim will get the message, but not feel disrespected.

Such an answer cuts out a lot of chitchat and still conveys your cheerful willingness to be helpful. At the same time, it announces that you are busy and want to get off the phone as quickly as possible. By not allowing Jim to defer and offer to call later, you will get the issue resolved quickly so you can return to productivity.

If encouraged to call back later, Jim may feel the green light to be more comfortable with the chit-chat when he thinks you are not in the middle of something. Further, letting Jim hear the "middle of something" speech two or three times in a row on the same topic may create unwanted tension between you. Get the business done with the fewest number of motions.

## Send A Memo

If Jim's request turns out to become more than you want to deal with at the moment or to create a face-to-face meeting, ask that he send you a quick email with a summary of the problem and the agenda for the meeting. It is just possible you can resolve Jim's issue by answering his message and avoid the time needed for a meeting or longer phone call, after all.

## New Patterns of Personal Behavior

When you start to set up systems and remove your avail-ability from your business, it could lead to the impression that you are not interested. You can avoid that impression by judiciously using your time to simply wander around.

Engage in light chat with employees and customers. Pay close attention to what you are seeing. Do not attempt to take corrective action during these tours – particularly if the people with whom you are engaging have a reporting relationship with a manager between you and them.

When you start to set up systems and remove your availability from your business, it could lead to the impression that you are not interested. You can avoid that impression by judiciously using your time to simply wander around. Engage in light chat with employees and customers. Pay close attention to what you are seeing. Do not attempt to take corrective action during these tours – particularly if the people with whom you are engaging have a reporting relationship with a manager between you and them.

You will be able to gauge attitude, adherence to established systems and whether the vision of the company is being expressed in the work you observe.

## Measure Everything

As your systems are established, much time will be saved if you know exactly what you are looking for. The famous quote from President Ronald Reagan, "Trust but verify," applies to businesses as well as international politics. There are a dozen or so key numbers that will tell you what is going on at the end of the period. It is important for you to be seen checking the numbers as they are being accumulated. It all gets down to the psychology of management. Let them know you care. They will increase their caring.

## Good Practice for The Future

Achieving The Objective will occur when you have diminished your need to spend time in the business just to ensure the business is operating to its maximum potential. Controlling the time your business and employees pull from you every day is good practice toward ultimately achieving it.

## CHAPTER 14

# How Do You Pick
# a Winning Team?

As your business grows and there is the need to "fill the boxes," there are many things to keep in mind as you do so. Much of what you need to keep in mind is embodied in the systems you have established and the obligations contained in the position descriptions described previously.

As you have developed your business, you have created, in your mind's eye, a living, breathing entity that is exactly the way you want it to be seen in the eyes of the world. It is this entity that will free you from the workaday world. It achieves The Objective of "working so you do not have to."

*Every hiring decision you make must reflect that vision in a way that supports it.* You must never accept an application from anyone who cannot totally support that vision no matter how desperate you might be for help. Much of your selection process will be with that vision in mind. It becomes the basis against which you compare all your hiring alternatives.

## But, I Already Have a Team

Those who are reading this text who have been in business for some time will, undoubtedly, have a staff already in place. This may or may not be a good thing. If you have a team that runs like clockwork and every single person fully understands and buys into your vision, and can help you get to The Objective, then you can skip this chapter.

If, on the other hand, you have uneven performance, non-workplace issues that impact performance or team members who cannot make a decision without checking with you, perhaps you should at least skim this one.

The fact is that agency owners who are committed to owning an asset often learn here that they need to make some significant structural changes. More often than not, staff who have been comfortable with the business "as it has always been" may not be part of the future of the institution. As difficult as that may be, it is almost always a part of the process.

This chapter will help you get in the frame of mind necessary to judiciously add to your team those people who can help you achieve The Objective. It will also highlight those who will slow your progress. Those must be your "subtractions."

## The Trouble with "Experienced Managers"

There is a great temptation to hire people with lots of experience to come in and bolster your team. In the interview with such people you will be seduced into the feeling that adding this level of experience will reduce your personal efforts and help your company grow faster. You might even get sold on the idea that you would be foolish not to hire them.

This feeling, however, is the first step toward the abdication of your responsibilities rather than your delegation of them. If the person is as good as he says he is in the interview, there is the great temptation to let him run with things after hiring him – because he says he can. And, since he has all this experience, you can assume that he knows what he is doing. Right?

Sadly, no. Building a business is far more than "getting the job done." Building a business is developing your vision of what it should be, not someone else's. The trouble with hiring experienced managers is that they have already been trained in *someone else's* way of thinking. They will start to tell you how to run the company. To allow that is abdication of your role as head of the company and, very possibly, allowing others to wrest your vision away from you. Be alert for the argument, "Well, this is how we did it at Groovy Nurses Home Care." You must *never* allow that to happen.

Alternatively, it is very possible to locate people who will buy into your vision and who want to become managers on your team. They will, of course, have some innate abilities that include home healthcare or hospice agency management as well as communication and leadership skills. They will not come into your world wanting to change it. They will absorb your vision and thoroughly understand that it is *your* company, *your* vision and *your* objectives. Agreeing to support what *you* want will get them the job, and the benefits that come with it.

This is possible because you will not be asking managers to manage *people*. They will only manage systems.

You will be asking the new managers in your company to manage the systems you have already developed. The *system* will manage the people. You do not need seasoned managers to try to outguess your systems. Your systems are exhaustively described in your *Operations Manual*. While you always remain open to great suggestions and new ideas, there is no room for reinterpretation there until you add those ideas to the manual. It is your manual. If a brilliant billing manager identifies a systems improvement, you should have a system for changing your systems. Here is where people with experience can be helpful. Follow the systems!

## Optimism:
## The Bane of Entrepreneurial Thinking

Entrepreneurs are inherently optimists. This is a problem. They tend to see the best in people. This occurs particularly in interviews when everyone is putting their best foot forward. Sadly, however, some people are incapable of grasping the vision of someone else and supporting it flawlessly, without trying to "improve" it. Or they simply reject it altogether and do what they want. They cannot be motivated or coached. Attempting to force this upon them leads to disappointment and resentment all around.

Guard against seeing candidates as you want them to be rather than what they really are. Having a system (that word again!) for the hiring process can prevent this mistake.

## Forget Ownership Thinking

One of the more common errors of wishful thinking is to assume you can select people who will "think like owners" of the business. You might have a compensation plan tied to success of the company and assume that it will cause everyone to pull together.

Well forget it! The only people who think like owners are *owners*. It really cannot be any other way. If your employees truly thought like owners, they would not be working for you, they would be competing with you in an agency they opened across town. Forever adjust your expectations that anyone will ever think like you. They can execute for you and uphold your vision. They cannot emulate you. They cannot think like you.

## The Power of the Written Word

You have been in situations where you are handed a standard contract with page after page of small print, such as when you bought a car or rented an apartment. You probably do not read it because it is "standard" and you certainly do not even think about changing a line because it feels (and may actually be) non-negotiable.

Having a written position description, complete with obligations, backed up by a written *Operations Manual*, can have the same psychological effect on your new hires. It will significantly deter the idea that your vision is negotiable and that how your company will be operated is subject to any interpretation. Using these written documents in the very first interview will assure that you will not lose control of the interview or the candidate before you can make a decision.

Obviously, significant push-back by the candidate makes your job of selection quite easy. Wish them well as you show them to the door. Conversely, you do not want to hire sycophants either. If you are vigilant, you will be able to spot the passive acquiescence a candidate might exhibit just to get the job.

## The System Driven Interview

There are thousands of books that offer a step-by-step process for conducting a job interview. These instructions are just fine for a large corporation that has a checklist of government rules they seek to obey and psychographic profiles they wish to match. They employ a system, just as you are being encouraged to do, and it works for that type of institution.

Yours, however, is a high-growth enterprise. That does not mean you ignore hiring or equal opportunity laws. It means that you are not looking for an automaton. You are looking for an executor; someone who can execute your plan using your Operations Manual exactly the way you have it written.

## The Hiring Process vs. A Selection System

Compare a typical hiring process with one that is a little "outside of the box" – a *Selection System*. First, let's go over the traditional "Hiring Process" that one such book suggests:

1. Review the applicants resume and note any points that need clarification or require more information.

2. Assemble statistics about the company to share with the candidate or to prepare for the candidate's questions.

3. Gain the candidate's confidence by being warm and friendly.

4. Scan the resume for a list of common interests you can discuss before getting into the meat of the interview to make the candidate more at ease.

5. During the interview, let the candidate do 90 percent of the talking. The Interviewer talks more only when describing the job responsibilities to the candidate.

6. Ask open-ended questions, not direct ones, to get the candidate to open up more.

7. Ask about work experience in chronological order from his last year in school.

8. Ask about educational experience, not just in terms of technical skills, but to ascertain the candidate's personality, motivation and achievement.

9. Describe the job using the job description. Ask the candidate how he will execute the requirements of the job.

10. Thank the candidate and give him or her some idea of when you will have a decision.

Now, contrast this approach with the *Selection System* process designed specifically to select the candidate that will lead you more quickly to The Objective:

1. Outline the attributes of the ideal candidate for the position for which you are hiring.

2. Review all applicant resumes and select those that exhibit the basic qualities and education to be considered further.

3. Invite all potential candidates to a group meeting at your office or public meeting facility such as a hotel meeting room.

4. In a formal presentation, describe the history of the company and your vision for its future.

5. Answer questions from the assembled group in a manner that confirms the commitment to your vision.

6. Narrow the list of applicants based on their appearance, perceived understanding of the company mission, quality of questions asked, observed interaction with other candidates and physical reaction to the message delivered.

7. After narrowing the field, meet with each surviving candidate individually.

8. Discuss his or her reaction to the description of your vision without reviewing the details. Observe the comprehension of your message in each candidate.

9. Discuss his or her background and experience and how they visualize themselves fitting into the vision as described. Listen for how the candidate fits him or herself into the vision. Be aware of those who suggest alternatives to your vision to match their own objectives.

10. Thank the candidate and give him or her some idea of when you will have a decision.

## Checking References

Once you have narrowed your choices down to one or two candidates, it is time for due diligence. You must assume that references offered by the candidate will be people from whom he or she is pretty certain you will get a positive report. It is, therefore, important in the process of the interview to secure the name of a candidate's supervisors in previous jobs. Just asking the question will provide some information about how the candidate left the last position. You should listen to what the candidate says, but reading between the lines can be useful too.

Assuming you can get a candidate's previous supervisor to speak with you given today's litigious environment, be aware that any separation can involve a personal as well as professional agenda. Here, reading between the lines is important too.

Speaking with more than one previous supervisor can give balance to your understanding of the candidate. Asking questions about impressions rather than specific actions may provide better insight. Feelings are sometimes more telling than facts.

## Decision Time

You have made your decision. Your top candidate did not have any dramatic skeletons in the closet and you are comfortable with his or her ability to understand and commit to your vision. You make the telephone call. The call is carefully scripted to make sure that the candidate enters the workplace exactly the right way. It is consistent with the entire selection process with careful reference to the vision of the company and the new employee's role in executing, not altering, that vision.

Carefully worded and thoughtfully considerate letters are sent to those candidates who are not chosen. Any of them could wind up in your pool again. A lack of consideration for their feelings can only hurt your company's image in the employment marketplace.

## The First Day

All too often the new employee is brought in on his first day and things become too casual too quickly. The new employee is shown around and introduced to existing staff, probably by nickname. Everything from work areas to computers to break rooms are shown off as you would to a prospective buyer or outside consultant whom you want to familiarize with your office.

In many cases, an experienced new hire may get little or no training, under the flawed logic that they were hired because of their experience and should know what to do already. The less the formality of this day, the greater likelihood that the new employee will not ever be fully settled and may ruin your investment by moving on much more quickly than had a more formal process taken place.

The *System Approach* to the First Day is different. It might go something like this:

The first moments of the first day are spent in your office. The vision is reviewed and the systems that deliver that vision are described, perhaps for a second or third time since the interviewing started.

The tour of the facility includes the standard tour and introductions, but the message is not, "Here is how we do things" but, "This is how our Systems work." As new systems are described, the way they intertwine is described as well.

Answers to the new employee's questions are handled in a forthright, not offhanded, manner.

Back to your office. Here the *Operations Manual* is delivered and reviewed with the new employee. Questions are answered. The formal statement of job responsibilities is delivered, reviewed and signed. Though the candidate has heard this information during the interview process, this is a formal document requiring a signature, signifying an understanding of the responsibilities and their relationship to the systems in place. This is not a job description and it is not an employment contract. It is a philosophical document that is consistent with the message delivered throughout the selection process and becomes the basis for the new person's employment.

Finally, the legally required government documents are executed for your files and payroll register.

## Do Not Fall in Love

The formality of the Selection System keeps a perceived distance and a respect for process. Sometimes, however, employees will come along and embrace the vision so well that they quickly become favored people in the workplace. It is critical for you not to fall in love.

First, favoritism will poison a work environment quickly. Second, relying too heavily on an individual who reflects your values so well can have a devastating impact upon that person's departure, should it come to pass.

The entire thesis of this book is building an institution that is independent of any one person – including you. Do not fall in love with individual employees.

Love the process.

## Do Not Overdo It

Even though finding the right people is much more challenging than finding too many, especially in the homecare business, the inherent loneliness of entrepreneurship tends to foment over-hiring. It is comforting having competent employees milling around. This is particularly true if they are selected as described above and all share a passion for the vision you hold for the institution. To some extent they become a cheering section for the boss and the business. It is infectious, and expensive.

Every new position that is filled needs to withstand the needs test. Does the institution need the headcount to grow? Non-growth expansion of staff is simply additional cost and a drag on achieving The Objective.

## CHAPTER 15

# If You Aren't There, Who's Going to Watch the Store?

In previous chapters, you should have gotten the point that the value of your business increases as your direct involvement in running it decreases. If, for some reason, you opened the book to this chapter and this is the first thing you are reading, here is a quick explanation: Your business only achieves a value when someone else is willing to buy it for its unique ability to generate a profit that exceeds what he will pay you for it. Obviously, you can own a business with value and not have to sell it. But deciding not to sell it essentially means you are willing to *buy it yourself.* To be valuable to someone else, however, since you cannot sell yourself (or your staff), you must develop a machine that is totally independent of all people – especially you.

## Flying IFR

IFR stands for Instrument Flying Regulations. This is the set of rules that allow a pilot to fly an airplane without being able to see anything beyond the nose of the plane. It makes flying possible at night, in clouds or heavy fog. It deals entirely with numbers calculated to tell the pilot about the status of his airplane.

The joke among pilots is that IFR-IGL for rookie pilots means "I Fly Roads – or I Get Lost." This means, of course, that a new pilot will use known roads or expressways as a hint to where he or she is in the sky. That is cheating – not to mention potentially fatal if the pilot ever really needs to get on the ground in a hurry after running into a cloud bank.

Lots of business people, attempting to extricate themselves from the day-to-day operation of their businesses, will do their own version of IFR-IGL. They cannot help themselves.

This chapter suggests that you fly your business strictly IFR. This means that you establish a core set of numbers – perhaps only eight or ten – that tell you immediately whether your airplane is sailing along smoothly, has hit a pocket of rough air or is heading straight into the side of a mountain.

## Your Key Numbers

In chapter 12, there was an example of a triage system for everyone who answers the phone. Out of the two dozen or so steps in the system, a single number emerged that would qualify as a key indicator of the status of the business, your conversion rate, the ratio of inquiry calls to the number of admissions.

You can measure the number of times your phone rings and know that your sales staff and Google reviews are working. You also know that phone calls are not revenue, and that your home care business is in much different financial shape if your conversion rate is 27 percent vs. 45 percent. It does not matter that one patient stays on service for a year and another requires only four visits. It is the average – to put is crassly – value per patient that you are measuring.

If your targeted conversion rate is 80 percent overall and one period it comes in at 70, this is a signal to look for the source of the problem. But if the numbers consistently fall within one point or so of your objective, there is nothing to do. If you are five points away, however, you must take the time to look for the problem. Look for things like vacations of key personnel, new hires not yet fully into your system, or even errors in how this month's rate was calculated. In any case, this single two-digit number tells you whether your airplane is on course or not.

Below are listed an additional set of possible key numbers.

- Gross Revenues vs. Forecast
- Total hours worked per pay period
- Total hours as a percentage of gross revenues
- Staff turnover for a measured period
- Billable hours by month, compared to year earlier
- Number of referrals by referral source, compared to year earlier

- Type of patient (profitable or net loss) by referral source (i.e. is one physician dumping patients on you that no one else wants)
- Quantity of client and family comment cards or Google reviews
- Satisfaction level average from feedback sources
- Average visits per day per clinician
- Age of receivables in days
- Number of consecutive PPS episodes (i.e. are you inviting investigator attention?)
- Monthly bank account reconciled (did it?)

These key numbers may be different for different operations, but you should be able to easily determine your own. If you have advisors, they may be able to give you guidance. Better still; compare notes with owners of other agencies whom you trust.

## Your Ticket to Freedom

When you have developed your systems and your key numbers, you will have achieved the next major step toward the reason you probably got into business to begin with: Freedom! (The Objective!) By being able to scan a sheet with ten or so numbers on it and know exactly where your business stands, you have the ability to either get back to the operation and start kicking the rear-end of people who should have fixed the problem before you even knew about it, or visit your next possible expansion city, potential strategic partner or, if you prefer, tee off on the back nine.

This type of organization also allows you to open additional locations with the same level of comfort. This represents your freedom to grow. This is entrepreneurism.

## Do Not Trust Your Gut

Suppose you are a fairly experienced pilot. You have flown in all types of weather and you have a good "feel" for your airplane. You have good "gut instincts" about what is happening while you are in the air. No matter how experienced you are, when you are in the middle of a cloud, you could very well be flying sideways, for all your gut can tell you. You always rely on the instruments – even if you think they are wrong!

All too often business people – particularly those with a bit of experience – will claim that they can make "gut" decisions and things work out alright. While that may be true, there are more than a few such businesses in the entrepreneurs' graveyard. Those with less experience die sooner.

Even if it does not damage your business, trusting your gut may have the effect of hampering business growth. Your gut may obscure opportunities if you know "too much."

Additionally, (harping on the same point again) you cannot sell your "gut" to someone else. So, let's use numbers, OK?

When it comes time to value your asset, having good, consistent numbers will dramatically increase the value of your business. A prospective buyer can gain comfort from knowing how the company operates and how he or she, with less experience, perhaps, than you, can run the business just fine without you.

## Business Devaluing Behaviors

It is probably more common than not. The owner of a small business is not taking a salary so he or she simply "borrows" from cash flow for "expenses." It becomes a steady flow of tax-free income over time. The legality of this strategy, tax-wise, is not our topic here.

Our topic is the powerful way in which this reduces the value of a company. In any sale, value is determined by a multiple of something. It could be a multiple of profits or a multiple of gross revenues. For most savvy business buyers, the multiple of gross is much safer. After all, it is very easy to reconcile the amount of money that does not hit the bottom line due to the owner being able to declare a salary of whatever he or she wants (legitimate payroll, not skimming), the "company car" and other "soft" expenses that have great latitude in the hands of a closely held business. When these expenses can be tracked, the prospective owner can calculate what the business "really" generates when you (and your car) are not in the picture. This allows the prospective owner to see clearly what money is available for hiring management and for compensating himself for his investment.

If it is agreed that a fair price for the business is 1.5-times gross revenues, a company selling $1,000,000 per year would sell for $1,500,000. (NOTE: This should not be any indication of what a "normal" sale arrangement would be in the business of Healthcare at Home. The ratio could be virtually any number based on industry and business history. The numbers used here are simply to make a point about skimming.)

For every $1,000 dollars that you "borrow" from the company cashbox, it reduces the value of your business (in this example) by $1,500.

Your safest route toward building a valuable, salable business is to treat it like an IRS auditor were sitting on your shoulder every minute of every day. It can be far better for you to take a salary even though employment taxes will take a bite out of you twice, once personally and once for the business. Someday, it may be important to be able to demonstrate total fiscal clarity for your enterprise.

If you have "clean" books, your value can be fairly and quickly established by a sophisticated buyer. If the books look "soft," your prospective buyer will sense that and discount an offer even more to cover the "fuzzy" things he cannot see in your books. Even if you never plan on selling your business, having a clean set of books is the best way to keep your options open. You never know what the next day might bring.

# CHAPTER 16

# Where is the Marketing Department?

Previously we talked about how every part of your business, from sales to scheduling to patient interaction to accounting, is really part of the marketing process. Virtually every function is visible to the customer in some way. To allow any employee or supervisor to operate without an acute awareness of your corporate image is severe mismanagement on your part.

Marketing is all about image and growth and everyone on your team is responsible. The Marketing Department is *everywhere*.

## "Good Afternoon!"

You see evidence everywhere of companies that understand that. As an experiment, locate a CMS five-star home health agency or a private duty home care agency with five stars from Google from their numerous positive client reviews. Call as though you are inquiring about their services. Chances are very good that you will get a friendly greeting and offer of help. Is this receptionist on the sales team? No, but is she on the marketing team? Absolutely. Does she know it? In this agency, she certainly does!

Contrast that with the last time you went to the post office or to the service department of your cellular provider. While there are notable positive exceptions, you have experienced those occasions where you were made to feel that your business was an interruption of their day, not the reason they are there to begin with.

Possibly this is because it is hard to find a competing letter delivery system and you are stuck in a two-year contract with your cell provider anyway. But, this should never matter. Not, at least, in the company you are building. Everybody is on the marketing team.

## The 5-Second Appraisal

When you enter a business for the first time, you get an immediate impression. In five seconds, you know a significant amount about the business, the owner, the people who work there and you make a mental assumption about the quality of the product you will receive from the transaction. Possibly, the better the place looks, the less price sensitive you become.

All of this happens without you even thinking about it. It is totally unconscious. You did not enter the establishment to conduct some sort of inspection. You came to possibly buy something. If the unconscious moves into the conscious, you might decide not to – or you might even decide you could become a long-term customer right at that moment. It is a powerful moment in time. It is that first impression. It can only happen once.

Now apply that knowledge to your own business. How do your nurses, therapists and aides look when they enter a home for the first time? Is their appearance professional? Do you even know? Is their equipment and the bag they carry it in new or held together with duct tape? You expect your outside sales people to wear business suits. Do you have a published standard for nurses? Do they look like nurses? Or like someone coming home from the gym?

## Employee "Rights"

Realize that this text is written to the owner of a business. Understand that the next statement will surprise some people. Others will understand it immediately. Your employees have no rights.

They do not have the right to "be themselves." They do not have the right to "dress for comfort." They do not have the freedom to gross out a percentage of your patients because they have elected to pierce parts of their face with metal decorations. Their "rights" cannot conflict with your marketing model; your image; *your vision*. They always, however, have the right to seek employment in a more casual type of business.

If your model, image and vision can accommodate a more relaxed appearance portrayed by your employees, fine.

Clinician comfort is why surgical scrubs were invented, wasn't it? Still, it is always *your* decision, not theirs. All too often employers get caught up in the notion that they must be "open-minded" about "young people." That is absolutely not true. Employees of any age must be "open-minded" about respecting the systems established by the person who signs their paycheck.

As you begin to remove the insanity from your business, you may remove people who will not conform to your new image. An Indianapolis-based restaurant called Steak-n-Shake has its policy in neon across the wall next to the kitchen. *"In Sight, It Must Be Right."* No one, whether customer or employee, can escape that bright red neon fact. Steak-n-Shake meant that for food, facilities and employees alike. The food is standardized, the facilities are impeccable and the employees are dressed in uniforms that match their jobs. None of them look like customers. Incidentally, there is a checklist on the back of the restroom doors proving that they were checked every half hour, and by whom!

With regard to your employees who are visible to the client or family member, they appear the way *you* want them to appear. If they cannot remove their piercings before work so there is no evidence that they exist, you have no obligation to hire or keep them. (We heard of an actual situation where a candidate got through the interview process before putting the ring back in his eyebrow and the employer felt powerless to do anything about it. He was not, in fact, powerless. The new employee essentially lied during the interview process.)

Think about the day when your business is finally for sale. What will the prospective owner think when he reviews your team? For example, does he see a group of employees in clean, company logoed outfits or a hodgepodge of randomly selected, "comfortably dressed" people? Every day between this one and that, your field staff, and your patients and clients, will be making the same observation.

The point? You developed the vision. You are the boss. Do your job!

## The Customer Is (Not) Always Right

The common saw that "the customer is always right" has the feel of a nice simple system, doesn't it? If the customer is always right, then the person representing the business in the transaction simply caves into whatever the customer wants. Nice, clean, simple – and wrong!

Customers are sometimes right. Regardless, it is the job of the person representing the company to make the customer feel right in any case. Usually, that is all it takes. From there, some fair resolution can be met. Letting the eldest daughter run roughshod over the situation can be expensive and debilitating to the morale of your staff. After all, the company is not wrong even though someone in your *company* might have been wrong.

This is where we get back to marketing. A comfortable resolution to a disagreement not only keeps the customer, but has the tendency to spread goodwill. People will talk more about a happy resolution than if nothing negative occurred at all. Treated properly, the customer will tend to empathize, cooperate and admire the company for its corporate "attitude."

## Strategic Relationships

No discussion of marketing would be complete without talking about strategic relationships. With payers pushing healthcare providers toward coordinated care, it is becoming a required business strategy – both for reasons of patient care and for competitive advantage – to communicate with acute care hospitals, rehab hospitals, physician practices, physical therapy clinics, hospices, long term care facilities and others. Perhaps the least expensive path to growth is to cooperate with other centers of care.

Less obvious, but equally important, are adult day-care centers, service organizations such as the Rotary and Lions Clubs, or local nursing schools that may be able to provide interns. Remaining open to partnerships can lead to cross referrals the same way they lead to cross selling in retail businesses. It is important, however, that your selected partners match up to the image you are trying to convey in your marketing efforts. Poor partnering selections can do more damage than good.

## Marketing Redefined

Most books deal with the mechanics of marketing. The four "P's" (Product, Place, Promotion and Price). In this text, we invite you to deal with marketing on a more cerebral level. View your company through the eyes of your customer (and ultimately the eyes of the prospective buyer of your company). You can nail down the mechanics of marketing and push as hard as you can. Without an intuitive look at how the market sees you, however, the effort may fall short of helping you achieve The Objective.

*Everything* is marketing. Plus, *everyone* is responsible – even your clients, if you ask them right. The next chapter covers that.

# CHAPTER 17

# Everyone's a critic.
# Respect them, Use them.

The term "reputation management" is widely used today. It is a term that is misunderstood on many levels.

On the most basic level, a staggering number of business owners simply have no idea that the concept even exists. The Internet world, and how it is impacting brick and mortar businesses, has literally snuck up on these business owners like a fog. They did not see it coming and most do not even know it is here.

Then there is confusion about the terminology. "Reputation Management" can be offensive or defensive. Most of this chapter deals with the offensive variety, where companies proactively do what is necessary to reflect the best possible public image through the words of those whom they serve.

Defensive Reputation Management is used when an event has (or maybe has not) occurred and the business is being criticized online by a customer (or someone who claims to have been one). Negative online reviews are usually the result of lack of attention on the part of a business owner or a member of the staff of a business. Rarely are they from maliciousness, though that does happen. In the homecare industry, negative reviews, more often than not, come from previous employees.

We will not spend much time on this topic, but removing negative reviews is a difficult and, often expensive, exercise. Unless a law or review site terms-of-service rule is broken, negative reviews cannot be removed. The only strategy is to ply the site with enough (legitimate) positive reviews to "bury" the negative report.

## You Do Not Have a Choice

Good or bad, you cannot "opt out" of the process. You do not have to sign up for anything, agree to participate or give permission. The fact that you exist with an address and a business phone number means that any person can go online and review your service. You do not have a choice.

What you can do is "frame" the reviews about your business. There are dozens of these review sites out there, but realistically only three deserve your immediate attention. They are Google, Yelp and Facebook. What is important is that the information you log with Google be consistent with every other site you can locate online. It is very important to "claim" your listing in each site that can include your business. "Claiming" is as simple as registering your business on each site with as much information and as many images as the site will allow. Claiming a larger number of sites with consistent data is also a key to helping Google find your business and rank it above others.

Perhaps you have gone to look up a company and the site where it is listed has a button that says, "Own This Business?" That means the owner has not "claimed" that site and is being invited to add information to it. If this shows on yours, always take the opportunity to do so.

This information on review sites is like free advertising, which is the best kind of advertising because it is not random. People who see you on review sites are specifically looking for home care services. This is how advertising is done today. Over 85 percent of people will look you up before they call you up – whether they saw your ads or were referred to you by people in their circle of influencers. At that point, they will decide whether to give you a call or not. That is why what is said about your agency online is of critical importance. That is Reputation Management.

## Inverse Marketing

The term "Inverse Marketing" is not a widely-known term today. This is good for you, actually. The fact that you will understand what it is and how to use it will give you a significant advantage over those in the home care business who do not understand its impact and importance. In fact, you will have what could be called an "unfair advantage" in your marketplace, simply by understanding the power of inverse marketing and applying it in a powerful way. Use it!

Marketing is telling prospective customers how good you are. Inverse marketing is getting your patients to tell strangers how good you are.

The old axiom was "Please a customer and he or she will tell a friend. Displease a customer and he or she will tell seven other people." Not anymore.

The Internet has changed all of that. Seven can turn into seven thousand. While a satisfied customer is certainly a good thing, a dissatisfied customer with an Internet connection can be a disaster. Today, an Internet connection is as close as a cellphone. The only real antidote is a dozen satisfied customers with an Internet connection and a motivation to speak up. A concerted effort to encourage those who are happy to express themselves and publish their feelings online is extremely powerful. Such an inverse marketing strategy will pay great dividends.

## It May Not Be Fair

An unhappy customer is dangerous. He or she can say just about anything and be protected by the concept of "free speech." There are cases of legal remedy for slander, but they are too few and too expensive to even consider. Just realize that you are subject to review by everyone with whom you come into contact.

Nor is an unhappy customer necessarily a fair reporter of the facts. Your side of the story is not going to be represented.

Sure you can reply, but you cannot edit. You cannot erase. Make no mistake about it, it is a dangerous world and will get more so.

Your exposure is even greater when you realize that your whole objective is to remove yourself as much as possible from daily operations. It means that one of the "systems" you must install will be a "culture infusion" to make every single person in your operation hyper-aware that every customer represents a positive advertisement or a devastating blow. One negative comment on a review site absolutely represents lost business. No one can relax when it comes to customer interaction in this new era of consumer reporting. No one.

## But It Is Not Illegal

Free speech is a wonderful thing but it can hurt too. Nowhere is this issue more prevalent than in the online review space. Consumers can say just about anything they like as long as it is not obviously slanderous and untrue. In such cases, "Terms of Service" for review sites will allow these types of comments to be removed. In fact, the business victim of slanderous reviews can even sue the writer – but not the publisher – of the review.

Of course, this assumes the writer can be identified. It can be a challenge to find out the real name of the writer of a review. Some review sites protect that information and getting to it can require court intervention. Again, an expensive option.

The publisher of the review cannot, generally, be successfully sued. The Communications Decency Act of 1996 had the original intent of "cleaning up" the Internet. The Supreme Court knocked out much of its intended objectives on free speech grounds. What is left, however, is a section of the bill (USC 47§ 230) that makes publishers of material written by others immune from responsibility for the content. This seeming unintended consequence of the law has consistently protected review sites like Google and Yelp from paying damages – even when real damage is the consequence of what they publish without responsibility for verification.

## Negative Bias

Compounding the problem is something called "human nature." People who do business with you expect to receive good service and quality products from you. It is the norm. Agencies which survive over time, by and large, deliver on that expectation. It does not, however, mean that satisfied customers are inclined to pull up a review site and write about an experience that they consider pretty normal.

But disappoint that same customer or make the experience exceptional in a negative way, and look out! These people will go out of their way to "warn" others by blasting you online. This behavior can be very dangerous and quite expensive for your business. People are far more inclined to say something critical than go out of their way to praise good service.

Part of your system must be to be vigilant in looking out for people who feel like they are not getting your best. Mistakes happen. People really understand that. But if they think you do not care, you will suffer badly. You cannot stop all mistakes, but you can usually stop a customer from expressing unhappy impressions publicly – if you have a system for hearing about it.

One such system is available that was specially built for the Healthcare at Home business industry. It involves the use of a client's cell phone at some point in the engagement when the patient or family member is expressing appreciation. The "favor" requested at that moment generates published reviews on sites like Google, Yelp and Facebook. In a world where few home care agencies are even aware that online reviews are available in their business, this little tip may make your reading of this book worthwhile by itself.

In full disclosure, this system was created by the authors of this book. More information can be obtained by visiting www.RowanReputationResources.com.

## Advertising Insurance

In today's world, you can spend as much as you want on advertising or community involvement to attract new customers, but still 85 percent of them will look you up online before calling for more information. Promotional activity will get your name recognized but reviews by past clients will tell the story. Thus, the term "advertising insurance." Time and money invested in bolstering your reputation online will dramatically improve the effectiveness of your marketing efforts.

It is, therefore, a total waste of money to advertise if you do not have your online reputation in a presentable form. It does not even have to be perfect. Five-star ratings are sometimes questioned as "too good to be valid." Conversely, having consistently fewer than three stars will keep new customers away in droves.

Adjusting to this new world gets back to the main thesis of this book: Systems. The establishment of systems to assure not only that customers are happy, but that a certain percentage of them are encouraged and motivated to say so online.

## Just Ask

It is not as difficult as you might think. Beyond making sure your operation is performing and managing the customer relationship proactively, the rest is easy. Just ask.

People may know how to leave reviews but they are rarely asked to do so. The mere fact of asking customers to leave an online review will do wonders – mainly because so few businesses do it. Not all, or even a majority, of customers will actually take time to leave a review, but the numbers will certainly increase over doing nothing at all.

Perhaps the most effective way to do this is to make it personal. Your staff can be trained to ask people to leave reviews "for me" in the form of a personal favor. People do not generally do things for a business, but they will do a favor for a person that they like. You could even reward employees when their names show up in reviews posted online. It is natural and comfortable for a customer to name a person in your business who stands out as being exceptional. And that is your goal.

The fact is, you do not need every customer to leave a review. (They will not anyway, but do not obsess over it.) If you can get two or three clients engaged every week, your number of positive reviews will skyrocket over other agencies. By focusing on asking a few patients or members of their families each week, the number of reviews will steadily climb – certainly far more than agency owners who do not ask. Systems such as the one referred to above can make the task dramatically simpler.

## Exit Strategy Considerations

By now you know the overriding focus of this book is not how to run an entrepreneurial business, but how to make it valuable as an asset. Lest you think that this conversation is all about marketing and growing or protecting sales, there is more to it than that. Valuation.

Due diligence by a prospective buyer can be broad and probative. But make no mistake, it is dramatically simple to do due diligence on online customer feedback. Businesses that have a larger number of positive consumer ratings, even if there are a few negative comments sprinkled among them, will be valued much more highly than those with little online visibility.

Historically, reputation had to be estimated from limited research about a business. Today it is easy to do and consistently a part of due diligence. Reputation is an asset and should be cultivated and protected as a valuable one.

## The Future of Marketing

At no time in history are businesses as exposed to the truth as they are today. The only surprising fact is that so few agency owners are aware of the extraordinary impact that reviews have on their business and its valuation. There is no going back. Management of your online reputation is the future of marketing – and ultimately the market valuation of your business.

# Chapter 18

# So, What Will You Do with All This Free Time?

You will know you have attained mastery over *Entrepreneurial Insanity* when you find you can stand back and watch it work; when you are invisible, to your staff when you have gotten past describing what your business does and moved on to where you can show off how it works.

As this book concludes, perhaps you have just begun. Know, however, that when you accomplish the task of removing yourself from the center of the action, you will have begun again. This time you will have truly begun your life as an entrepreneur, leaving the mantle of "small business owner" behind. You are the fly on the wall, invisible but present. You get to watch what is happening through the tiny peephole of a dozen numbers electronically delivered to your smart phone wherever you are in the world. You will know at a glance that your patients are safe, your software is working, your staff is efficient, and your healthcare at home business is flying accurately.

So, what will you do with all this free time?

Will you grow the business through sales in a way that only the owner can? Will you examine weaker (or stronger) competitors with an eye toward acquiring them to increase your size and market share? Will you nurture partnerships with other healthcare providers in your market area, such as those mentioned in the previous chapter? Will you take the systems you developed and replicate them in an entirely new, but parallel, business in another location? Any of these activities can grow your wealth based on the security you have gained by establishing systems that replaced you as the key ingredient in your first business.

What else will you do, now that you can? Will you take your spouse on that long vacation you have promised since the day you opened the doors? Will you write trade magazine articles instead of just reading them -- that is, when you had time to read? Will you volunteer in your community, both as a way to give back and as a way to be exposed to those who will want to do business with you?

Perhaps you will attend more state and national association conferences, or even join one of their boards, where you can drop the seeds that result in people knowing that, under the right circumstances, your business is "in play" and could be purchased at the right price. Whatever you do with your newfound free time, once you have developed your plan and followed it, you will enjoy all the freedom you deserve.

Congratulations! You have accomplished The Objective. You have been forever transformed from small business owner to *Entrepreneur*.